Recipes

Interviews

Production
Neil Rippington
Red Cherry (Bristol) Ltd
neil@redcherry.uk.com

Rebecca Saunders
Red Cherry (Bristol) Ltd
rebecca@redcherry.uk.com

Area Key:

- South West
- Wales
- London & East
- Midlands
- Scotland & North

www.thegreatgameguide.com

Foreword

By Glynn Purnell

TV Chef & Chef Patron at Purnell's Restaurant

It's that time of year again. From the 'glorious 12th' of August until the splendorous last day of the season on the 1st of February. It's all about that one amazing food type... GAME.

For those who eat, cook and understand this tremendous ingredient, they can enjoy it throughout this joyous and fruitful season, and have a true understanding of what a pleasure it is to cook, eat and serve. And for those who have not yet been exposed to such a treat, you truly have a wonder to discover. I love game. The menus, throughout season, write themselves. Or do they?

When cooking game, a lot of cooks and chefs will always turn to the classic and traditional methods of preparing and serving. The likes of venison with Grand Veneur sauce, mallard with orange, and pheasant or partridge served with game crisps and bread sauce are all traditional and delicious dishes. But as the UK has become more diverse, it has put a whole new perspective on what I choose to serve with game.

Having been brought up in Birmingham, in a very multicultural and exciting city, I have brought my love of game into a fusion of what my city and country now represent. A curveball of cooking has emerged on my own menus, just like with many other like-minded chefs. My take on venison is now with an orange, sichuan and ponzu gel; I do a radical duck with almond satay and a crazy Pheasant Maryland with - yes, rub your eyes - a banana. And that's how exciting game can be.

So here it is, guys. By all means, stick to the traditional and you will enjoy it. Hang it, or don't hang it. Whatever your preference. The big thing is, sometimes you have to throw the rulebook away, spread your wings (pardon the pun), and experiment. Just as you would with a chicken breast or a pork chop.

So, from the bright summer morning of the 'glorious 12th' of August to the cold, crisp, frosty morning of the 1st of February, don your apron, drag out your pots, let the sparks fly, think outside the box and enjoy this monumental harvest. You may even find yourself pulling out a banana.

PURNELL'S

Photo credit: Patrick Hendry - Unsplash.com
the great game guide
2021/22

Introduction

By Chandos Elletson

The tradition of eating game in this country dates back centuries and no other set of ingredients are so fiercely anticipated every year from the Glorious 12th of August to the end of January.

The game season, once it begins, does not remain the same as the months progress and this is what makes it so special. Younger game tastes very different early in the season to how it does by the end. This canvas of flavours is what chefs love about it.

But that's not all. Game can be cooked simply to bring out its unique set of characteristics but, equally, it can become a launch pad for a new set of flavours and ideas. This is what The Great Game Guide is all about.

We love game in all its forms and we are excited to introduce a new guide to eating it, buying it and discovering it. So, in the middle of this guide you will find our 100 top eateries that specialise in game.

Some of these are fancy, some are not. Some like to cook game classically, others are more adventurous. You'll find chefs who love it spicy alongside others who only cook it simply. And you'll find pubs next to restaurants and hotels.

The Great Game Guide is a melting pot of ideas, cultures, styles and techniques but every single listing is united in praise and enjoyment of this wonderful part of the British gastronomic year.

I very much hope you enjoy the guide and the game content we have put together. But more than anything I hope you enjoy the six months of the game season!

Chandos Elletson - Editor

game varieties

Wild ungulates (hooved animals) lagomorphs (rabbits and hares), and wild birds that are hunted for human consumption are collectively known as 'game'.

Game Birds

PHEASANT: The pheasant is a large game bird, characterised by the long pointed tail. The male colourings are very variable, but typically they have a copper body plumage with a glossy dark green head, scarlet wattle and white neck ring. The females are about two thirds smaller than the males and duller in colour with plumage tones varying from light to dark brown.

PARTRIDGE: The grey partridge is a native British ground nesting bird. Wild grey partridge have declined over time and they are also the focus of concentrated conservation efforts within the shooting community. Shooting is part of that management and takes place if there is a sustainable surplus.

WOODCOCK: The woodcock is a bulky wading bird with short legs, and a very long straight tapering bill. Woodcock are a mainly nocturnal wading bird, which inhabits damp woodland with open rides.

SNIPE: The Common Snipe can be found in marshes, flooded meadows, bogs and moors and is more prevalent to the South West than any other region of England. It is a migratory bird, which is small and stocky with a long beak.

PIGEON: The wood pigeon has been native to Great Britain for centuries. The wood pigeon is easy to recognise; a delicate grey overall with white wing bars and, in the adults, a white neck band.

WILDFOWLING: Wildfowling is one of the few truly wild shooting experiences in the UK, which involves shooting mainly migratory ducks and geese on marshes and estuaries around the coast. The most common are the mallard, teal, wigeon, pintail, shoveler, gadwall, tufted duck, pochard and greylags.

GROUSE: A medium to large game bird with a plump body and feathered legs, the male being larger and more brightly coloured than the female.

Deer is the most common ungulate in the South West although some wild boar is also hunted. The South West has several species, which are hunted:

Deer

RED DEER: Red deer are the largest wild deer in the UK, and one of our native species. There are substantial populations around the South West including Exmoor and the Quantocks.

SIKA DEER: This species is believed to have been introduced to Britain in the 19th century, but is originally from Asia. Intermediate in size between roe and red deer.

FALLOW DEER: During Mediaeval times many deer parks that held fallow deer were established and these and more recent park escapees have given rise to the free-living populations in Britain today.

MUNTJAC: The muntjac is the smallest species of deer resident in the UK and originates from Asia. They are still relatively rare in the West Country - but you could be lucky enough to spot one.

CHINESE WATER DEER: These deer are native to China and North Korea where their natural habitat is river valleys and lowlands. They were first kept at London Zoo in 1873 but escaped from Whipsnade Zoo after introduction there in 1929.

ROE DEER: Roe deer is Britain's most abundant deer. It is a native British species which is thought to have died out in the South of England during the Middle Ages, however the population has since re-established itself.

Rabbit & Boar

RABBIT: Rabbits do untold damage to crops, fields and threaten livestock with their digging. They can be found almost anywhere where there's a supply of edible fodder. Rabbits are a recognised agricultural pest throughout the West Country.

WILD BOAR: The wild boar is the ancestor of the domestic pig. After an absence of 300 years wild boar are back in the English countryside and have strongholds in the Forest of Dean in Gloucestershire, Devon and Dorset.

The Great Game Map

You can find evidence of game pretty much everywhere in the UK countryside but certain areas have more variety and density when you take into consideration the prevailing landscape. If you are new to game then this very basic map will help you understand where the best game areas are.

In conjunction with our list of regional restaurants, you can expect to find dishes and ingredients that largely line up with these areas. So, for example highland red deer is an obvious association but the wetlands of west Lancashire for duck may not be. Equally you'll find an abundance of woodcock in Wales and great pheasant shooting all down the southern corridor of counties from East Sussex all the way along down to Devon and Dorset.

The great grouse moors of North Yorkshire and Perthshire are perfect environments for that type of shoot and are highly prized. You'll find fallow deer in abundance in the central counties of England.

The UK has the perfect landscape for game. Forests, wetlands, moors, valleys and hills. It's wet, windy and timeless when you get out into the natural areas far away from civilisation. It's there that game thrives and what makes it so enthralling for those who have never experienced it.

the great game guide
2021/22

Anatomy of a shoot

Marc Brown - Bettws Hall Estate Gun Manager

What makes a good shoot great?

The very pinnacle of shooting is a soaring pheasant flying high on a cloudy November morning with a gentle breeze. On Brigands, one of the shoots that is part of the Bettws Hall Estate in Snowdonia, that's what you'll be presented with. A day on this shoot will consist of 4 drives, each with hospitality in between, magnificent scenery and some of the most exhilarating shooting imaginable. But, for the very best shots, this is what game shooting is all about.

The birds are up at a challenging height, they're travelling at an extraordinary speed and your gun is at near its limit. In other words you've got to be a competent shot. The bird stands a chance. A typical drive lasts in the region of twenty five to thirty minutes and, according to Bettws Gun Manager Marc Brown

"You can be left breathless! It's hard work!"

A lot goes into creating this shoot with fore-knowledge of the team of guns an advantage.

"We like to know the ability of those who are shooting and what they are looking for. At this level, guns appreciate the importance of an unforgettable shot they can talk about later than simply just sheer number of birds in the bag. But, it's not easy to create. We have to make sure that the birds are at the right height and speed. This means the beaters have to present the birds in a certain spot so that when they are flushed they have the time to get to the preferred height. If you are too early they will be too high, and too late and they'll be too low. It's a skill. All I can say is that you won't forget the experience in a hurry."

This level of shooting is as good as it gets.

BETTWS HALL
Sporting Estates

Photo credit: Charles Lamb - Unsplash.com

Anatomy of a stalk

Donald Mackenzie - Arinecknig Estate, Strathcarron, Highlands

You know you are in the right hands when your deer stalker tells you that pulling the trigger is not the best bit of stalking. A really top deer stalker will tell you that the fun and the thrill of stalking is all about getting into position.

"Deer have three senses that make stalking very difficult," explained Donald Mackenzie, Deer Stalker on the Arinecknig estate in the Scottish Highlands. "Their eyesight, smell and hearing are phenomenal and they frighten easily. They have the odds in their favour.

"So, stalking is about getting into position, understanding wind direction and not being in any hurry. But it's also more than that. It's about finding the right deer to shoot. We don't just shoot any deer we come across. There's a good reason aside for the sport and that's to keep numbers under control.

"Stalking is culling and we do this because the land where deer roam can only sustain a certain size of herd and if left alone they will die of starvation which is a form of animal cruelty. So, as deer stalkers we are highly selective.

"I've found a perfect deer shot within 10 minutes before now but on closer analysis we've had to back away because the deer we found were too good to be shot. This is an important consideration but backing out of a shot can be just as exhilarating as crawling in. The goal is for the deer to never know you were there.

"If the deer sees you or hears you there is a chance, if you are very careful and still, that they will settle again but if they smell you then they are gone and nothing will bring them back. Stalking is about knowing the wind and getting into position. But the wind can change. Stalking is not for everyone but it can be a fantastic experience for those that cherish the hunt."

John Queen

Head Gamekeeper at Linhope Estate

"For inspiration I look at Formula 1. Game keeping is all about aerodynamics."

"A gamekeeper is an old-fashioned term that has been around for generations but it doesn't fully describe the job or necessarily the person in the job.

A great example of this would be John Queen, head gamekeeper at Linhope Estate in Northumberland. It's a title that he feels is a bit outdated because of all the other work he does like conservation and land management.

However, under the hood, is a man who lives and breathes to produce the best game birds for the season and that means examining everything that goes into getting a bird into the air at speed. To do this he spends some of his time studying Formula One.

"Game keeping is all about aerodynamics. Those racing cars need speed, fast. It's the same with a game bird. Think of it like this - a pheasant can only fly at top speed for between 8-10 seconds," he explained.

"It's aim, when driven from cover, is to get high. High enough to be safe. The bird is flying for its life. Every ounce of its wing strength goes into those seconds. If it makes it and survives then it will be asked

to do that same flight again later in the season, if not the following week. My job is to make sure it has the right nutrition from the start to give it the strength it needs to fly.

"To do that I look at everything from nutrition to bone density and even barometric air pressure on shoot days. I spend a lot of time with a friend who is technical director at Red Bull Racing, the Formula 1 Team. I've studied aerodynamics

"Northumberland has been described as one of the last pieces of true wilderness in the UK"

and why it is so important for the birds to have the right fuel and that's where we start.

"We haven't used antibiotics in any of our birds for 8 years. Their diet is rich in protein when they are young because they need it to grow but later when they need energy it's all about maize. This plays a major part in their energy levels and gives them a fighting chance of survival. And that's what its all about - great shooting is a skill and the birds need to be given the correct food to get into the air fast.

"On any given day we have to choose the exact spot from which to launch the birds and where to place the guns. We need a little bit of wind but not too much and air pressure is important. If it's too heavy the birds will struggle so they have to be higher or the guns lower. This is where the precision of the job comes in.

"Beyond that game keeping is about land management, ecology and preservation. Where I work in Northumberland has been described as one of the last pieces of true wilderness in the UK.

That's part of its appeal. That's why people come here and say it's some of the best shooting they've ever had. Yes, they want good shooting and our birds are exceptional but in reality they want more than that. They want to be standing somewhere special, taking in the landscape, the air, the history and finally, for those mad minutes, the thrill of pitting their wits against the speed and power of the birds."

Photo credit: Andrea Cairone - [illegible]caironejpg

Green Shoots

How The British Association of Shooting and Conservation (BASC) is helping to preserve both countryside and wildlife.

For over 20 years, the BASC has been working with the shooting community on a really valuable project known as Green Shoots. This effort, which enables land owners who use their land for shooting to map out how they use it and this is helping conservation.

"People know that our countryside, and the wildlife it supports, is under increasing pressure - but how much more pressure would there be without the influence of shooting sports? Nearly £250 million is spent on conservation every year," the BASC says.

"The BASC strives to have this recognised by politicians, the media and the public. One way we do this is by working with the shooting community and partners to target conservation efforts on land which is shot over, in order to achieve public conservation targets. We call this programme of work Green Shoots and it is extremely successful in linking shooters and non-shooting conservation organisations for the benefit of all wildlife.

"Green Shoots was launched in the House of Commons in 2000. It gave BASC the framework to record what species and habitats of national importance could be found on members' land. Members were then given the opportunity to work with partners on projects that achieved public conservation targets.

"Initially information was collected in certain areas through paper surveys and this inspired some highly successful and respected projects. Now all BASC members can provide useful information on their shooting land and the wildlife it supports by using the Green Shoots Mapping website.

"Green Shoots is endorsed by Natural England, Natural Resources Wales, Scottish Natural Heritage, the Northern Ireland Environment Agency and the Environment Agency (which covers England and Wales). This shows the strong support BASC and the shooting community have for their conservation efforts."

To find out more visit the BASC Website: basc.org.uk

BASC
The British Association for Shooting & Conservation

Game Standards

Why you can be certain that the game you buy meets very high standards.

The end result of any shoot or stalk is a customer. It is important for everyone to understand this. Though the image of shooting may be sporting the fundamental fact is that it is a food source and nothing else. Birds or animals are not shot purely for the sake of it. They are shot to be eaten and there are very clear rules that have been laid down by organisations such as **The British Game Alliance (BGA)** that make sure this is taken very seriously. The future of shooting and game is entirely dependent on eating.

However, behind the scenes, there are also clear rules on animal welfare and the safety of the general public. Shooting and stalking are very carefully governed and this is a good thing. The purpose of the BGA is to promote the consumption of game. The BGA Standards cover the marketing of game and ethical issues which relate to consumer confidence.

The Code of Good Shooting Practice sets out the framework that enables shoot managers, guns, gamekeepers and their employees to deliver sustainable shooting whilst paying attention to the management of habitat and avoiding nuisance to others.

It is not in the interest of the shooting industry to flaunt these rules and so customers can be assured that every precaution has taken place to deliver a first-class product that is safe to eat, nutritious, free of unregulated medicines or antibiotics and wild in every sense.

If you want to read the **BGA standards guidelines** and discover more about the governance of shooting and stalking visit their website: **www.britishgamealliance.co.uk**

BEST PRACTICE BEST BRITISH GAME
BRITISH GAME ALLIANCE
FOR THE FUTURE OF GAME

Photo credit: Vincent Van Zalinge - @vincentvanzalinge

Mike Robinson

The Woodsman Restaurant, Stratford-Upon-Avon

www.thewoodsmanrestaurant.co.uk

"Why we must celebrate venison and do the countryside a favour?

Deer populations have become larger due to Covid, the closure of restaurants and stricter rules on stalking and culling. What was a population that was becoming untenable is now getting out of hand and could become a big problem for the countryside.

So says venison and game lover Mike Robinson, who's company **Deerbox**, is leading the charge to get people to eat more venison.

"It's really simple! We need to embrace wild venison. It's actually a win win situation. The meat is delicious, there's plenty of it, it's not a strong flavour or bloody. It's high in protein, low in cholesterol, it's sustainable and carbon positive.

The problem with deer in the wild is the damage a large population does to the forest floor. Deer eat up young trees and saplings and prevent forest growth. If this is not halted there will be an effect at some time. But the deer themselves are not the enemy. It's important that we all understand that. Deer are an asset to the countryside and the community".

"The answer is to promote the eating of venison. This way the populations will come down as a consequence. This guide is an excellent place to start. It contains lots of restaurants and suppliers where you can buy game and venison and that's what is needed.

"One of the really wonderful things about wild venison is that it is versatile. It really is the best meat you can possibly eat. Game has a reputation for being strong and over-flavoured but actually that's not true. Venison has a unique meaty flavour that tastes of the woods and countryside.

It's wonderful to cook with as there are so many different cuts. It makes a great steak but also a terrific braise. I encourage you to eat as much of it as you can!"

www.deerbox.co.uk

Curtis Pitts

Curtis Pitts Deer Services, Langlands Farm, Devon

“Deer expert Curtis Pitts talked to The Great Game Guide about the process of stalking and handling a deer carcass and why it is so important and the key points that must be done properly.

Assessment and shot

"We go out and assess different herds of deer in parcels of land to select cull animals to harvest," he explained. "We do this to improve herd health and population density. We don't want the herd to become too big.

"Once the animal is selected we have to stalk / approach it silently to get into a position where it is safe to take a shot. The aim is to get in as close as possiblé to prevent error and to be as humane as possible. Stalking must take place within daylight hours for legality, but dawn and dusk are preferable for deer behaviour as they are more active.
How long does it take?

There is no given time factor on a stalk. They are a wild animal and the factors can vary for every stalk.

Sometimes it can be quick stalk and a cull animal can be easily selected. On other occasions it can be a struggle to find a cull animal. This all comes down to knowledge of the land and the local deer.

What happens after a deer is shot?

Once a deer is shot and down it becomes a food product. The first thing that happens is an initial inspection of animal health. It is important to confirm that the animal is dead. Once that is clear then the carcass is hung to drain as much blood from the carcass as possible. Then the stomach, large intestine and small intestine are removed and inspected. Processing back at the larder can now begin. ”

Interview

Hywel Griffith

Beach House Oxwich
www.beachhouseoxwich.co.uk

"Welsh born chef Hywel Griffith is the perfect expression of a game loving chef. He hunts and shoots and trained in kitchens that take game seriously - The Chester Grosvenor, Ynyshir & The Freemasons at Wiswell. Now he has a Michelin star at The Beach House in Oxwich on the Welsh coast.

We caught up with him to get his thoughts on game and game cookery.

"Game to me is a fantastic, diverse and sustainable British product from Partridge, Rabbits, Grouse all Othe way up to the largest wild mammal we have in the UK the Red Deer. To me as a chef it's important to follow seasons as that's when produce is at its best (I mean why would you cook an ingredient when it's at its poorest condition?).

"I am myself a hunter. I stalk deer and wild boar and take a few mallards and geese. Game meat is brilliant for cooking. It's healthy and it has a low carbon footprint. Its rich in iron, vitamins, high in protein and very low in fat - aside from wild boar.

BEACH HOUSE
RESTAURANT

"However, when it comes to hanging game, I believe this is where game meat gets a bad rep. I have witnessed all sorts of methods, some have been good, some have been horrific. For me small game and birds should be hung a week give or take a few days.

"Muntjac and roe need 7-10 days. Fallow, Sika and reds 10-14 days all hung in fur/feather before they are prepared.

"Also don't eat Bucks/Stags when they are rutting - the meat is tough and has an odd taste that will put people off. A Doe/Hind generally makes far better eating.

"Don't forget that game is wild and anomalies can happen, be prepared to change menu at short notice if something isn"t available!"

TOM HILL SCULPTURE
www.tomhillsculpture.co.uk
Stunning Metal Animal Sculptures to beautifully-adorn and Enhance your Business or Property
Traditional Metal Craft and welding techniques using recycled horseshoes
Elegant life sized sculptures of animals large and small
Commissions Welcomed
Tel 01438 717336 I Mobile 07886 928789
tomhillsculpture@gmail.com
© 2017 Tom Hill Sculpture

John Williams MBE

Executive Chef, The Ritz Hotel, London

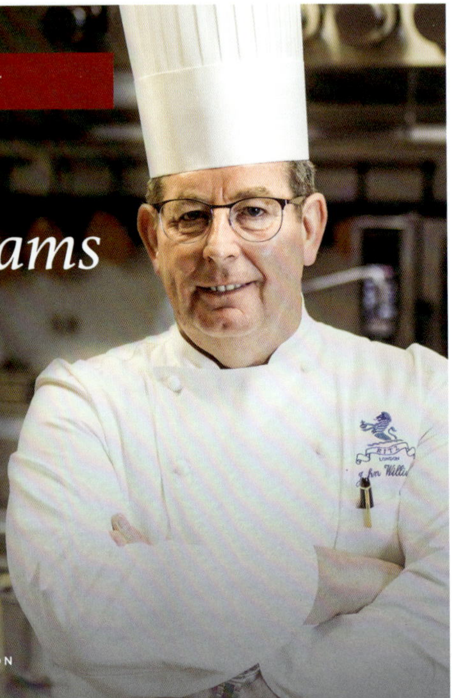

THE RITZ LONDON

“My love affair with grouse didn’t start that way

John Williams heads up the most traditional kitchen in the UK: The Ritz Hotel and its iconic restaurant that overlooks Green Park. If it’s grouse your after the minute the season starts then look no further if you want the best. John Williams likes game but he loves grouse. However, as he tells The Great Game Guide - it didn’t start out that way.

“My first job in the kitchen was plucking and gutting grouse and did not have a clue what it was as I came from the sea side it was in a court yard and I felt sick with the aromas. However, I learned to love the aromas and 40 years later I went back to where my first job was and looked in the courtyard and my memory went straight back to the 21st august 1974.

I had an out of body experience of seeing my self plucking and gutting the grouse with all the aromas. It was quite emotional and if you ask anyone what happens in my kitchen on the 12th of August I am anxiously waiting for the first delivery so I may get that first wonderful aroma of the grouse and heather.”

“Game is massively important to me in our kitchen. I love wild food because it has a natural flavour that comes from the natural environment which gives it a distinctive flavour and seasonality.

“On the question of hanging I believe it is an important part of the process. I think it was overdone in

the past but it has a part to play in breaking down the enzymes in the gut of the bird which will tenderise the meat.

This takes between four and seven days before gutting to make sure it is ready for butchering and cooking.”

ESTABLISHED
1935

Real Fruit. Real Flavour.

FOXDENTON
SPIRITS & LIQUEURS

It all starts with the fruit, and at Foxdenton we have been sourcing the BEST from British Farms since day one. Our mission, and the key to our success, has been to find and support Farms that share our passion for quality.

We offer a full range of bespoke products to our customers, from Own Label House Gin for Gastro Pubs to Branded bottles of Fruit Gin for Shooting Estates.

We work closely with our clients to understand their needs and tailor an offer specific to them. This can include anything from corporate gifts to full scale unique products development and brand ideation.

Whatever your needs we can find a solution.
We look forward to working with you.

For more information please visit our website.

FOXDENTONESTATE.CO.UK

Lisa Goodwin-Allen

Northcote Manor, Lancashire
www.northcote.com

"Lisa Goodwin Allen inherited a kitchen at Northcote Manor which already had a fondness for game and all things local. Lisa worked under the founder of Northcote, Nigel Haworth and became accustomed to working with the best ingredients that the North West has to offer.

But, when it came to game this was a subject she knew well. She grew up with it and shared her father's love of cooking it from an early age.

"I can remember my dad bringing home a brace of pheasants from work and my Nan would also cook them all the time. I loved the whole romance of game being something that came in all shapes and sizes and you never knew what would be next.

"What I love about game is its versatility. You really can take in any direction you want. Of course, there are classic, time-honoured recipes and I love them. But sometimes when you go out to dinner at somewhere like Northcote you are looking for a new experience and that's what we do.

"The rack of venison is a show-piece and a good example of our approach. I did it on the Great British Menu recently. It's a herb-crusted rack of venison, venison sausage, game chips, bread sauce and mulled beetroot. It has classic elements with a new twist.

"At Northcote we get a lot of duck coming in. It's part of the region and what we're known for. So teal, widgeon and wild mallard are pretty much always around. I feel very privileged to cook with them. These are species I didn't come across as a child. The other thing we see now, which is really special, is snipe.

"One thing I have noticed is that grey-legged partridge are less common than they used to be. What we get comes from the Yorkshire moors. They are spectacular and so different from the red legged ones."

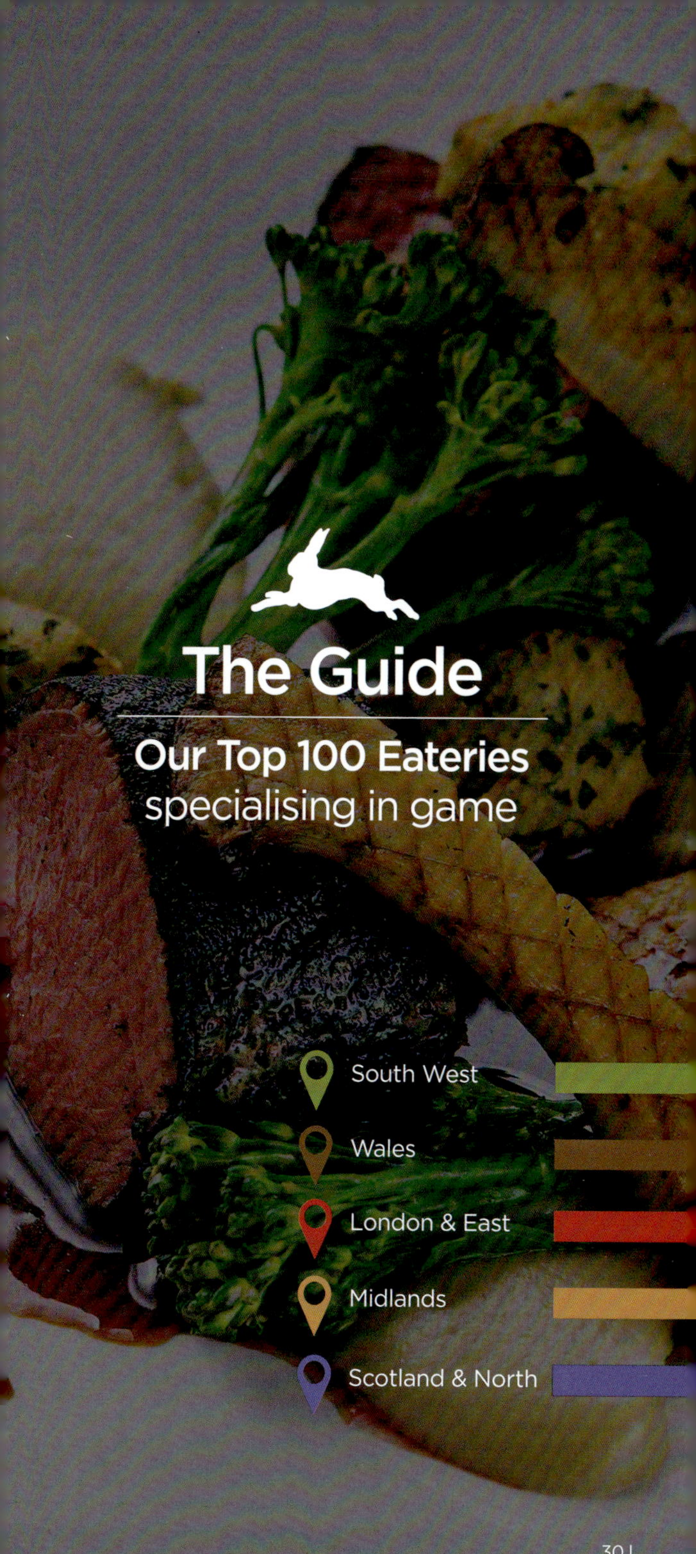

The Guide

Our Top 100 Eateries specialising in game

- South West
- Wales
- London & East
- Midlands
- Scotland & North

Bank House

Wine Bar & Kitchen

Kent

Owned by former CEO of Gordon Ramsay Restaurants Stuart Gillies and his wife Cecilia, Bank House in Chislehurst is a new-style hospitality experience that offers accessible luxury without the fuss.

A newcomer on the restaurant circuit it opened at the end of 2019. Gillies also worked for Daniel Boulud in New York as well as for London restaurateurs Corbin and King.

Expect high standards and delicious food with game getting the respect it deserves.

Stuart Gillies
Proprietor

Getting to now

Stuart Gillies career highlights:

- Lord Byron Hotel, Rome
- Daniel's. New York
- Le Caprice, London
- Angela Hartnett at The Connaught Hotel
- Boxwood Café, London
- The Grill Room, The Savoy Hotel
- Plane Food, London Terminal 5

www.bankhousechislehurst.com

11 High Street
Chislehurst
Bromley
T: 020 8249 0461
E: office@bankhousechislehurst.com

Benedicts

Restaurant

Norfolk

Game lovers will love Benedicts primarily because the chef, Richard Bainbridge, is so classically trained. His CV includes stints at the 3 Michelin star Waterside Inn in Bray under the late Michel Roux OBE and at Kevin Thornton in Dublin. Local to Norfolk he was head chef at Galton Blackiston's Morston Hall.

So, expect the game dishes on the menu to be seasonal and treated with thought and care. Bainbridge runs the restaurant with his wife Katja and is well known to fans of Great British Menu as a winner in 2015.

"The full flavour and real, natural, sense of seasonality of game gives you a real sense of time and place as it changes from region to region. A connection with a natural product with real foundations is brilliant for any good chef".

Richard Bainbridge
Chef Patron

www.restaurantbenedicts.com

9, St Benedicts Street
Norwich
NR2 4PE
T: 01603 926080
E: info@restaurantbenedicts.com

BENEDICTS

Berwick Lodge

Hotel & Restaurant

Bristol

Once you visit Berwick Lodge you won't forget it. Perhaps the only way to describe it is that's a bit mad but in a brilliant way.

Primarily, Berwick Lodge, run by owners Sarah and Fevzi Arikan, is a hotel but the kitchen is its beating heart. Head chef Istvan Ulmann is a lover of game and it features on the menu throughout the season.

"I love Autumn.I love the strong flavours of game, particularly hare, pigeon and venison. Nothing beats a hearty game dish as the weather turns colder."

"I feel being from and working in the South West, game is a important yet underused produce from our doorstep. The versatility and unique flavours are the some of the reasons I use game on my menu. I feel it is important to showcase the wonderful produce this amazing country has to offer."

Dan Bowden
Head Chef

www.berwicklodge.co.uk

Berwick Drive
Bristol
BS10 7TD
T: 0117 958 1590
E: info@berwicklodge.co.uk

BERWICK LODGE SINCE 1890

Boisdale Belgravia

Restaurant

London

Boisdale has a huge cult following. It's described as a lively Scottish restaurant in Belgravia, London and is situated in an old Regency townhouse.

There's a cigar terrace, a whisky bar and live jazz every night. But that's not the secret of this institution. Here's where you'll find all your old favourite dishes done in the old-school way.

If you're after grouse on the 12th August and you want to enjoy it the way it once was then head here. You won't be disappointed.

Colin Wint
Head Chef

Menu highlights

Carpaccio
Juniper Cured & Smoked Wild Venison Morels, truffle mayo, rocket, parmesan

Venison Burger
Venison shin ragu, triple cheese, truffle mayo

www.boisdale.co.uk

15 Eccleston Street
Belgravia
SW1W 9LX
T: 020 77306922
E: info@boisdale.co.uk

BOISDALE

Interview

Jose Souto

Senior Chef Lecturer in Culinary Arts at Westminster Kingsway College.

"There are few truly wild ingredients left to us as chefs and we should be excited and look forward to the first day of the season and beyond when we can, for that short period of time, get our hands on these most wonderful ingredients.

I take game very seriously. I am lucky enough to shoot my own game and I hunt with a Peregrine and Goshawk. Falconry is one of my main hobbies. I also do a lot of deerstalking so during the season I get to harvest quite a few deer for the larder. At home we eat venison at least 3 or 4 times a month.

Game is so varied. There are 7 different birds species and over 10 different Wildfowl (Ducks and Geese) species not to mention Hares, Rabbits and the 6 deer species in the UK. All of these present different problems and opportunities but one thing is in common with all of them - you need a good set of knives.

When I was writing my two Game Larder books I wanted to use good quality, reliable, knives. I discovered and fell in love with the range from Flint and Flame. Their selection of knives cover every area of the kitchen and look the part.

The Game Larder collection of knives are specially put together to with a view to helping chefs and foodies alike prepare, cook and get the best out of their game. Flint and Flame are always innovating and developing their knives with a look to giving quality fit for purpose and that's why I recommend them to everybody to use - especially when working with game."

Westminster Kingsway College

Bowood Hotel

Hotel, Spa & Golf Resort

Wiltshire

Bowood has a golf course and a spa but it also has fine dining in that quintessentially British way located in a fine old country house.

The Shelburne Restaurant, headed up by chef Rupert Taylor, is modern and relaxed and the perfect place to come for a stay and a good dinner.

Game is treated with care and attention and served with imagination. The menu is constructed in the classical way so you can expect high quality ingredients that shine. You'll also find a strong wine list and excellent service.

"Game is amazingly versatile with lots of different ways of cooking to extract different flavours. I love to showcase the game we have here on the estate and the surrounding areas. Game can be tremendously challenging to prepare and cook correctly but also brings great joy when done right."

Rupert Taylor

Executive Chef

www.bowood.org

Derry Hill
Calne
Wiltshire SN11 9PQ
T: 01249 822228
E: resort@bowood.org

BOWOOD
Hotel, Spa and Golf Resort

Photo credit: © Steve Lee

the great game guide 2021/22

wk Westminster Kingsway College

Venison Epigrams

by Jose Souto *Senior Chef Lecturer in Culinary Arts at Westminster Kingsway College*

Epigrams of lamb are good but venison ones are even better they have more flavour. The boned-out breasts are cooked slowly until tender in a well-flavoured stock with herbs and wine but they can also be cooked sous vide in wine and herbs for 13 hours overnight at 75°C then pressed. This dish can be eaten as it is or as part of another venison dish.

Wine Pairing *See page 165*

Ingredients Serves 4 - 6

- 2 boned out breasts of venison to the weight of about 2 kilos.
- 1.5 litres venison stock or brown chicken stock
- 2 glasses red wine
- 1 medium onion
- 1 medium carrot
- 1 clove of garlic
- Sprig of thyme
- ½ bay leaf
- Salt and pepper as required
- 100g Dijon mustard
- 2 eggs
- 200g plain Four
- 200g fresh or Japanese breadcrumbs
- Oil for deep frying and frying off veg

Method

1. Roughly chop onion, carrot and garlic
2. Place some oil in to a deep pan large enough to take the venison breasts.
3. Heat oil and then fry off onion for 5-6 min. Now add the rest of the vegetables and herbs and cook for further 5-6 mins then add the wine and reduce by half.
4. In a separate pan, bring stock to boil.
5. Place breasts on top of the herbs and vegetables, season them and add boiling stock then bring back to the boil slowly.
6. Reduce the heat to a simmer and cook for 2-3 hours or until meat is tender. When the meat is cooked you should be able to take it in-between your finger and thumb and as you pinch, your fingers will go through the meat.
7. Once meat is cooked, take out of stock and allow to cool slightly for 10 mins.
8. Place one of these still just warm breasts onto a sheet of grease-proof paper on a tray and then place the other breast on top, covering with another sheet of paper. Place a weighted tray on top of both breasts and put in fridge to chill overnight.
9. Once chilled, remove the paper and carefully place the breasts onto a chopping board. They should have become loosely bound together.
10. Trim and square off the whole breasts then cut into portion sizes. These could be squares, triangles or rounds.
11. Once you have cut them, place a wooden toothpick into the centre of each portion. This will help you to pick them up and the portions will hold together during cooking. Holding the pieces by the toothpick, brush them liberally with Dijon mustard then pass lightly through flour, tapping off any excess. Next pass through beaten egg and then through the Japanese breadcrumbs, making sure that all the areas are covered in the breadcrumbs, still holding them on the toothpick.
12. Heat the oil to 170°C and carefully lower the Epigrams into the oil with the toothpicks standing up, fry until golden-brown then drain, remove toothpicks and serve

Interview

Pierre Koffmann

BBC Maestro and Former 3 Michelin Star Chef

"

What does game mean to you?

Game to me is beautiful wild meat and fish that lives in its natural environment such as grouse woodcock and venison and hare as some examples.

My first job in the kitchen was plucking and gutting grouse and did not have a clue what it was as I came from the sea side it was in a court yard and I felt sick with the aromas however I learned to love the aromas and 40 years later. I went back to where my first job was and looked in the courtyard and memory went straight back to the 21st august 1974 and I had an out of body experience of seeing my self plucking and gutting the grouse with all the aromas . it was quite emotional and if you ask any one what happens in my kitchen on the 12 th of august I am anxiously waiting for the first delivery so I may get that first wonderful aroma of the grouse and heather!!!!

Why do you like it so much?

Game is massively important to me in our kitchen I like wild food and it has its natural flavour coming from its natural environment giving distinctive flavour and seasonality and very healthy lean meat! The very distinct flavours and seasonality being with us for short periods its precious.

What's different about game when you cook it compared to regular meat?

It is very lean meat it should be looked after when cooking certainly with an amount of fat in the process and never over cook .

How do you feel game sits on a menu? Is it perceived as a luxury?

It is certainly a luxury its limited and season I and we should treat all game as such we always have game on our menus in season .

Do you feel game encourages you to be creative or traditional?

I believe it s both I will cook some very traditional but we are always looking to evolve our cuisine and come with new dishes but cook with classic elements.

What is you favourite game? How do you like to cook it?

Grouse or woodcock are my favourites grouse with ceps and blackberries or woodcock a very traditional lightly roasted A la fine champagne with truffles.

When you eat game out - what do you go for?

Grouse venison snipe .

Should game be aged or hung?

This is a great question game should be hung and served fresh some of the problems we have had with getting people to eat game was because they feel they were not getting fresh meat ,the hanging process is nothing other than to allow the enzimes in the gut to tenderize and flavour the meat for between 4 and 7 days and then once gutted this is finished and ready for butchering and serving.

What are you looking forward to putting on your menu come August/ September?

Grouse without doubt

"

Calot Manor

Hotel & Spa

Gloucestershire

Chef Richard Davies continues to impress with his careful balance of Modern British and Classical French at Calcot Manor's Conservatory restaurant.

Davies trained under Gordon Ramsay at Royal Hospital Road and also at wine lovers favourite The Vineyard at Stockcross. At Calcot, a spa and hotel in the Cotswolds near Tetbury, his clean flavours and attention to detail bring nuances out of the best ingredients.

Expect game on the menu to be cooked with precision but presented in a new way.

"I love using game at Calot, I love the game season with the hearty and robust winter flavours, game is also very healthy as it is often very lean and low in fat and cholesterol. The animals are often local, the carbon footprint is low therefore having a better impact on the environment!"

Richard Davies
Executive Chef

www.calcot.co

Calcot
Nr. Tetbury
Gloucestershire GL8 8YJ
T: 01666 890391
E: reservations@calcot.co

CALCOT & SPA

Carters Of Moseley

Restaurant

West Midlands

Brad Carter is a no-nonsense chef inspired by producers who work the land.

The restaurant, near Birmingham, aims to treat ingredients with the upmost respect and admiration by reconnecting with the rhythms of farming and foraging by championing ancient preservation techniques and by celebrating whole animal butchery.

Brad works closely with producers around the UK to preserve cultural traditions and harness the heritage of fruits, vegetables and rare breeds of livestock with direct links to wild animals. Basically, when he does game it gets done properly.

Brad Carter
Chef Patron

Did you know?

Carters also sells a range of their own salt available through the website:

- Sea Truffle Droitwich
- Charcoal Droitwich
- Coastline Droitwich

MICHELIN STAR

cartersofmoseley.co.uk

2c St Mary's Row
Wake Green Road
Moseley
Birmingham B13 9EZ
T: 0121 449 8885 E: enquiries@cartersofmoseley.co.uk

carters of moseley

Roast Loin of Roe Deer

with Perl Las Cheese, Bacon, Pear & Jerusalem Artichoke

BEACH HOUSE
RESTAURANT

By Hywel Griffith Head Chef at The Beach House Restaurant,

Ingredients Serves 4

- 350g piece of roe deer loin
- 50g good quality pancetta
- 1 ripe pear
- 25g white balsamic vinegar
- 150g Jerusalem artichokes
- 250g milk
- 80g Perl Las cheese
- 1 ltr chicken stock
- 200ml red wine
- 500g roe deer trim
- 1 onion
- 1 small leek
- 1 carrot
- 1 celery
- 1 garlic
- 5 junipers
- 1 sprig thyme
- 50g sherry vinegar
- 25g honey

Wine Pairing See page 165

Method

Start with the sauce, take the deer trim and fry in a deep sided saucepan until evenly browned, add the chopped onion, carrot, celery and leek, keep frying on a high heat until the mirepoix has browned, add the honey and allow that to caramelise, now deglaze with the red wine and reduce until almost all the wine has evaporated, now add the chicken stock, crushed junipers and thyme, simmer for an hour skimming any scum off the top. Pass the sauce and discard all the solids, add the vinegar and reduce by ¾ pass once again to remove any sediment.

For the puree, peel and dice the artichokes, place in a pan with the milk and season, simmer until the artichoke is just starting to fall apart, blend and pass through a fine sieve.

Dice the pancetta small and fry until crispy and golden, drain from the fat and set to one side for now.

For the pear simply peel and cut either side of the core, vacuum pack in the vinegar and allow it to sit for at least an hour. Roast the roe deer loin, aiming to keep it medium rare, allow it to rest before carving.

Chez Bruce

Restaurant

London

It is hard not to be effusive about Chez Bruce and the cooking of its owner chef Bruce Poole.

For starters the restaurant itself was the once legendary site of Marco Pierre White's Harvey's. But since1995 it has been a restaurant all of its own.

A serenely classic dining room that exudes charm with food to match. At Chez Bruce you will find classic dishes that don't need to try hard.

The menu is perfectly created and has no pretensions beyond wanting to be excellent and delicious. Game Chez Bruce will be memorable.

Bruce Poole - Getting to now

After several years working front-of-house Bruce Poole started cooking professionally in his mid-twenties as a junior chef at Bibendum Restaurant, London in 1990. A year in the kitchen at The Square followed, and after that he worked at acclaimed restaurant Chez Max as sous and latterly Head Chef.

MICHELIN STAR

www.chezbruce.co.uk

2 Bellevue Road
London
SW17 7EG
T: 020 8672 0114
E: enquiries@chezbruce.co.uk

Chez Bruce

James Martin

TV Chef and Restaurant Owner

"I really can't stress enough how important it is for chefs, cooks and restaurants to utilise more of the amazing selection of game we have access to in this country.

There's such a variety to choose from and the secret to its fabulous taste is in the simplicity of its cooking. There's something out there to suit every pallet too, from fresh early season partridge and grouse, to the stronger venison and other feathered game later in the season.

Game will continue to feature heavily throughout the season in all my restaurants, as it always has done. Both my chefs like to cook it and our customers can't get enough of it!"

james MARTIN

www.jamesmartinchef.co.uk

Claude Bosi at Bibendum

Restaurant

London

Bibendum is a classic London restaurant created originally by the late Terence Conran. The first head chef was Simon Hopkinson and the food and the decor have always managed to set trends.

Claude Bosi, best known for his previous 2 star restaurant Hibiscus, is now in charge of the kitchens and you can expect brilliantly conceived dishes from his extensive repertoire executed with skill and panache. If there is one room in the UK to sit back and enjoy game it would be at Bibendum beneath the beautiful stained glass windows.

"The game season is, for me, the highlight of the year. It is a natural showcase of autumn and winter. Hare is a great favourite of mine and on the feathered side it has to be woodcock- it is truly wonderful!"

Caude Bosi
Head Chef

MICHELIN STAR

www.claudebosi.com

Michelin House
81 Fulham Road
London SW3 6RD
T: 020 75815817
E: enquiries@claudebosi.com

CLAUDE BOSI

Cliveden House

Hotel, Restaurant & Spa

Berkshire

Cliveden House sits above the River Thames in Berkshire near Taplow. The countryside melts away into the distance making Cliveden the country house hotel that seems to set every standard.

Inside Roux Scholar chef Paul O'Neill continues the culinary excellence that defines Cliveden's heritage serving up seasonal, classical, food with British ingredients.

No expense is spared bringing in the best and with that view from the dining room there could be no finer place to enjoy game. O'Neill worked with Pierre Gagnaire in Paris so you can expect food with some unique twists.

"Game season for me is a wonderful time of year. It gives me the opportunity to expand my repertoire and utilise different ingredients that aren't always available.

For me fallow deer has to be my favourite as I find a challenge in all the different cuts. This might it be slow cooking and braising the haunch or mincing the shoulders for pies, suet puddings and pasta fillings. Alternatively I love to gently cook the loin."

Paul O'Neil

Executive Chef

www.clivedenhouse.co.uk

Cliveden Road
Taplow
Maidenhead SL6 0JF
T: 01628 668561
E: reception@clivedenhouse.co.uk

CLIVEDEN

Coworth Park

Hotel, Restaurant & Spa

Berkshire

Coworth Park has a lot going for it. It's part of The Dorchester Collection, set in its own grounds and is formidably exclusive. But there's another reason to get excited about a visit to this relatively new hotel on the luxury circuit: chef Adam Smith.

For those not in the know Adam Smith completed his entire training at The Ritz under John Williams. It's rare for a chef to do that but Smith is an exceptional talent and his food is a combination of the classical and the modern. Coworth is a great game secret.

"Game is a very British thing and I am deeply passionate about cooking with British ingredients.

What I love about the game season and cooking with game is that it is so versatile and allows you to be very creative: from paté en croute, terrines, charcuterie all the way to simple roasting, poaching and braising. The list is endless."

Adam Smith
Executive Chef

MICHELIN STAR

www.dorchestercollection.com

Blacknest Road
Sunningdale
Ascot SL5 7SE
T: 01344 876600
E: info.CPA@dorchestercollection.com

COWORTH · PARK
ASCOT
Dorchester Collection

Crockers Henley

Restaurant

Oxfordshire

Crockers Henley is an interesting concept which offers a number of unique dining experiences, and rooms, under one roof on the river at Henley-on-Thames.

There's a Bar & Grill headed up by Tom Westerland and two very different chefs tables where you'll find Alex Payne (Thames) and Iain Dixon (Gardiner).

That's three opportunities to discover various styles and flavours of game which features throughout the season. Each chef's table has been designed to create a sense of theatre with a direct view of it's dedicated kitchen. The Bar & Grill features its own charcoal grill.

"British game is at the forefront of British produce and my ethos on food here at Crockers is great food starts with great seasonal produce and great produce starts with great farmers."

Tom Westerland

Head Chef of The Grill

www.henley.crockersuk.com

20 Market Place
Henley-on-Thames
Oxfordshire RG9 2AH
T: 01491 529837
E: hello@crockershenley.co.uk

Crumplebury
Green Cow Kitchens

Restaurant

Worcestershire

Set in the heart of the Herefordshire countryside and surrounded by woodland, green fields and happy animals Crumplebury was the name of Whitbourne Estate's old pigsty. The 18th century red brick build remains at the centre of what is now the fine-dining restaurant, **Green Cow Kitchens**. In winter the menu features estate pheasant, partridge and duck. The team of chefs forage for wild garlic, hedgerow berries, damsons, plums, apples, pears, puff balls, elderflower and more. The monthly tasting menus celebrate the seasons and reflect what is ready and at it's best from the farm.

"Whether it be a whole venison, pheasant, rabbit or partridge from our 1,500 acre estate, sustainable game is a frequent addition to our menu. We are lucky to be in such a prime area with an abundance of wild game available."

Stuart Banks
Head Chef

www.crumplebury.co.uk

Crumplebury Farm
Whitbourne
Worcester WR6 5SG
T: 01886 821632
E: hello@crumplebury.co.uk

Crumplebury
For the curious

Gary Maclean

Winner of Masterchef The Professionals 2016

Gary Maclean won Masterchef The Professionals in 2016 and is now Executive Chef of the City of Glasgow College and Scotland's National Chef.

We asked him what game meant to him.

"I am a huge fan of game," He began. "My earliest memories of starting out in hospitality was working with game. I first started my career at a very good country house hotel situated very close to Loch Lomond. The kitchen was always full to the brim with the most incredible produce, from red deer, to pheasant, snipe, hares and Roe deer as everything from the local shoots came directly to us."

"So being surrounded by this volume and range of what was on our door step was amazing. At 15 years old I thought this was the norm of all kitchens and to be learning the skills in how to handle it was an incredible experience."

Years later his opinion has not dimmed.

"I feel you can use game in any application, it works well whatever direction your imagination takes you. Game has changed over the last 30 years, the route to market has become like clockwork, and they tend to get processed much quicker giving a very consistent and regular product that the industry can rely on. This has given us products that are not as strong and gamey as they once were."

Would you perceive it now as a luxury?

"Game can most definitely seen as luxury, but I feel there is a shift coming, with people's concerns with health and environment, game is a perfect meat to eat more regularly and just to touch on its versatility you can make loads of midweek meals from game, I am a big fan of making things like venison burgers and meatballs for the family. You get a magnificent flavour from using minced venison in all sorts of traditional family meals."

Fhior

Restaurant

Edinburgh

Fhior is a new addition to the Edinburgh restaurant scene and was opened in June 2018 by Scott and Laura Smith, with the vision to create a dining experience wholly reflective of the word Fhior which means "true" in Gaelic. That means being true to Scottish produce and producers, true to an ingredient's flavour and seasonality, and true to the artistic expression of the team.

The dining experience delivers a constantly evolving set menu, showcasing the season's produce at its best and taking you on a journey through Scotland's culinary landscape.

"Game is ubiquitous with Scotland. Our customers expect it and we love cooking with it.

The raw element of romance with a wild product is especially exciting as it is straight from nature and we usually take it in its full form.

This offers the team a chance to get to grips with game butchery - we use absolutely everything and nothing is wasted."

Scott Smith
Chef Patron

www.fhior.com

36 Broughton Street
Edinburgh
EH1 3SB
T: 0131 477 5000
E: info@fhior.com

fhior

Galvin Green Man

Pub & Restaurant

Essex

The Green Man is a pub done by the Galvin brothers, Chris & Jeff who have been at the top of the London restaurant scene for close to twenty years. It was a natural progression for them to consider opening a pub.

The result is set in the Essex countryside, close to Great Waltham in a building dating back to 1341. There are great views as well as an extensive garden. And the brothers grew up nearby so the place means a lot to them. You'll find all the usual Galvin touches including renditions of game classics done in their unique style.

Chris & Jeff Galvin
Chef Patrons

Did you know?

The Green Man dates back to the 14th Century and the River Chelmer runs by at the back. The Chelmer flows through Essex and runs for 40 miles from the north west through Chelmsford to the River Blackwater near Maldon.

www.galvinrestaurants.com

Howe Street
Great Waltham
Chelmsford CM3 1BG
T: 01245 408820
E: betty@galvinpubco.com

GALVIN GREEN MAN HOWE ST.

Simon Wood

Manchester Chef and Restaurant Owner

Manchester chef and restaurant owner Simon Wood (a former Masterchef winner) grew up with game and learned to love it from an early age. We asked him why game means so much to him.

"My earliest memory is my grandma teaching me how to cook Rabbit Stew when I was ten," he began. "I used to stay with her every weekend. I was amazed that you could actually cook rabbit as we had them as pets at home. It was one of my first fond memories that actually drew me into cooking. "It's rabbit and that's what you're having" she said and I wasn't bothered at all! I loved it."

We asked Simon what he's making at the moment.

"Right now I'd say that wood pigeon is my favourite. I love what game offers in terms of inspiration. We do a little game tartlet with confit mallard legs and we use all the offal from the pigeon through that. It has red currants in it for acidity and we dust the top with a fermented red cabbage powder and baby thyme leaves.

"As a garnish we make a lamb bacon out of lamb breast - this is a twist on the classic pigeon and bacon. On the side is a Marmite-infused sour dough, then we render the fat out of the lamb fat so it is liquid. We then fold it through the bread sauce to give it a real umami flavour.

"Game is so unique - the colour, the flavour and where it comes from. I love that it's wild and full of natural flavour. It is so deliciously different. It deserves respect and you need to be careful how you treat it and buy it."

"The thing with game is to not be scared of it, just give it a go."

www.woodrestaurantgroup.com

Galvin La Chapelle

Restaurant

London

Brothers Chris & Jeff Galvin are known as two of the most hard-working and talented chefs in the country. Both have chef CV's from the very top of the industry. Jeff learnt his craft alongside Marco Pierre White whilst Chris worked for years with Terence Conran.

Their mixture of French brasserie classics and British flair is on show at Galvin La Chapelle where the food shines under Jeff's direction. His ability to take the heart and soul of every dish to new heights is a mainstay of the London restaurant scene.

Chris & Jeff Galvin
Chef Patrons

Fact!

The building which houses La Chapelle is a former chapel built in the Victorian age when Spitalfields was less than desirable. It became synonymous with Jack the Ripper who's victims where all from the local area.

MICHELIN STAR

www.galvinrestaurants.com

35 Spital Square
Spitalfields
London E1 6DY
T: 020 7299 0400
E: elise@galvinrestaurants.com

GALVIN
La Chapelle

Hambleton Hall

Hotel, Restaurant & Spa

East Midlands

Hambleton Hall in Rutland is, according to Tom Parker Bowles: "A legend in the world of country house hotels, not just for its longevity but for its obsession with excellence". It's a fair assessment and diners can expect beautiful renditions of game dishes in season.

Chef Aaron Patterson has been head chef since 1992 and so knows the style of the hotel and it s philosophy well. He started at Hambleton Hall in 1984 and then left to work in other kitchens such as Raymond Blanc and Anton Mosiman before returning.

Aaron Patterson
Head Chef

The site of Hambleton Hall lies in the middle of what is now known as Rutland Water. This man-made lake is a reservoir and was constructed in 1975 by damming the River Gwash. Two Hambleton villages now lie under the water.

MICHELIN STAR

www.hambletonhall.com

Hambleton
Oakham
Rutland LE15 8TH
T: 01572 756 991
E: hotel@hambletonhall.com

FAYCE QUE VOUDRAS
HAMBLETON HALL

Hare & Hounds

Pub & Restaurant

Glamorgan

A 300-year old pub in The Vale of Glamorgan which offers a daily, changing, seasonal menu that features game alongside ingredients from the Vale and from the kitchen garden. Everything is made from scratch in the kitchen, from sourdough bread and cultured butter, to fresh pasta.

Chef Tom Watts-Jones grew up locally and remembers playing in the pub garden. He trained as a chef in London at stalwarts The Anchor & Hope and the Michelin starred St. John. Now he's back to promote the very best of Welsh food.

Tom Watts-Jones
Head Chef

Did you know?

The Hare and Hounds has its own bakery which was born out of the first lockdown in March 2020.

The pub was well known for its bread and started life as a food trailer borrowed from a friend.

www.hareandhoundsaberthin.com

Maendy Road
Aberthin
Cowbridge CF71 7LG
T: 01446 774892
E: info@hareandhoundsaberthin.com

HARE & HOUNDS

Stevie McLaughlin

Head Chef at the Two Michelin Star Restaurant Andrew Fairlie

Chef Stevie McLaughlin was the long-standing head chef at Restaurant Andrew Fairlie before the sad passing of his mentor and friend Andrew Fairlie. There was no finer or better prepared chef to take over the running and direction of the restaurant. Stevie McClaughlin embodies everything RAF stands for. We asked him why game is so important to him and the restaurant.

"Game plays its part in the essence and the heritage of my country," he began. "The Scottish moors, hills and forests provide an abundance of life along with life-sustaining beauty. When I cook game I always get a sense of where it comes from. In other words what its natural habitat is and what its typical diet is, too. I get a real sense of what each and every animal's natural place is in the ecoculture. Whether this is when I am plucking and drawing a grouse and I can smell the bitter wild berries and the purple heather or I'm boning out a shoulder of wild roe deer and I can actually smell and appreciate the aroma from pine trees, flowering plants and brambles.

"Game also changes through the season. A great example of this is grouse. It's not the same at the beginning, in August, as it is at the end of the season in January. Young grouse needs something tender like a leafy vegetable and maybe a puree of caramelised mango flesh and a warm game vinaigrette spiked with a few drops of homemade wild berry vinegar. However, towards the end of the season when grouse becomes a more pungent offering you would expect to see it on our menu with roasted cepes, celeriac puree perfumed with clove or nutmeg and a much more robust game jus possibly flavoured with a peaty malt whiskey.

andrew fairlie

www.andrewfairlie.co.uk

Hart Street Tavern

Pub & Restaurant

Oxfordshire

Hart Street Tavern is the second instalment from David Holliday & Alex Sergeant following the success of their country pub with rooms, The Bottle & Glass Inn just a few mile away - Hart Street is their take on a modern British tavern in the heart of Henley-on-Thames. Taking its inspiration from Danny Meyers Gramercy Tavern in NYC.

With Joe Bartlett at the stove, Hart Street Tavern is all about local produce cooked seasonally with care, skill and understanding, a bustling bar & cocktail scene sits alongside an extensive wine list and with regular live music on the in-house grand piano it really is a focal point of the Henley dining scene.

"Game plays a huge part of what we offer here at Hart Street Tavern. It features daily from the start of the game season, right up until the very end. It's so important to embrace and not only make use of it but to perhaps inspire others to do the same."

Joe Bartlett
Head Chef

www.hartstreettavern.com

38 Hart Street
Henley-on-Thames
Oxfordshire RG9 2AU
T: 01491 876800
E: hello@hartstreettavern.com

hart street TAVERN

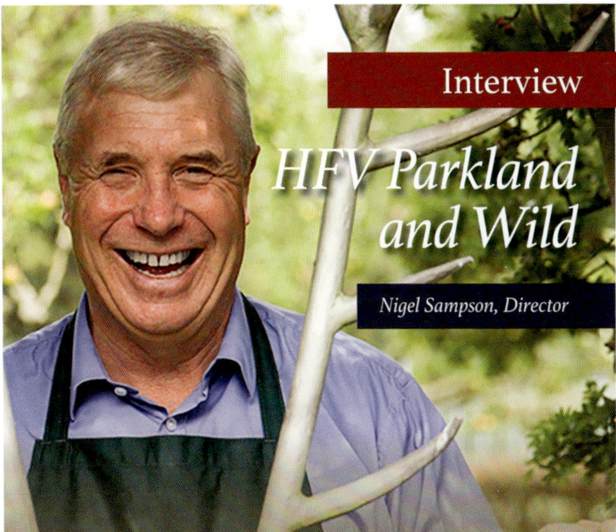

HFV Parkland and Wild

Nigel Sampson, Director

What makes HFV Parkland and Wild (HFV) so special ?

Through an interest in food and farming as a complete circle, we identified the opportunity initially to sell the finest quality Venison from our farm. This path led us to meet the needs of today's customer, who wants something local, well-butchered to the standards of any other meat, but most importantly using some of the natural deer species that flourish in our countryside in the UK. We are proud to champion this as the most natural and healthy food of all, natures sustainable, from deer that roam our woods and fields right across the country.

Why have you launched the new Parkland and Wild Brand?

HFV 'Parkland and Wild' is our new brand of fully traceable wild venison that will meet the public demand to make the most of our native wild deer in Britain. As the name implies it is seasonal, British, wild venison and the best from many of the ten wild species of deer that roam freely in and about our natural UK countryside. With Venison's natural qualities being one of the healthiest meats available, we believe this has led to something of a 'game renaissance' and HFV have stepped-up to the mark to provide our consumers with the species choice they are looking for from Farmed, Wild and Organic Venison.

Why do your customers benefit from the best of both worlds?

In selling quality Wild, Organic and Farmed Venison in our online shop, it allows us to offer 'the best of both worlds' to our customers for whatever their preferences may be. By converting our naturally species-rich grassland to carry organic status, it is a natural progression from what we have already been doing on the farm for years.

Our special organic range is available for a few glorious months of the year due to limited supply. Our wild venison is available all season and both are available to buy in our online shop for delivery to your door.

Harwood Arms

Restaurant

London

Hidden away in the back streets of Fulham, the Harwood Arms offers award-winning food and wine in a casual and relaxed setting. Chef Jack Leach champions the very best British produce with a focus on game and wild food.

The Harwood is currently the only Michelin-starred pub in London. It is part owned by game enthusiast Mike Robinson and also by Brett Graham who ran The Ledbury before it closed.

Dining at The Harwood is unique in that simplicity and ingredients are married with technical skill to create something new.

"I feel British game is undervalued, even though we are so lucky to have such flavoursome, wild and sustainable produce on our doorstep. We put a lot of effort into incorporating game into our menus to encourage people to enjoy it, as well as using it in their own cooking."

Jake Leach
Head Chef

MICHELIN STAR

www.harwoodarms.com

Walham Grove
London
SW6 1QP
T: 020 7386 1847
E: info@harwoodarms.com

Heaneys

Restaurant

Glamorgan

A stylishly laid-back suburban restaurant in Cardiff run by chef Tommy Heaney. Opened in 2018, the restaurant quickly received praise from critics and guests.

Heaney has worked for chef luminaries including Richard Corrigan, David Everitt-Matthias, Ollie Dabbous and Nacho Manzano at Casa Marcial in Spain. Heaneys has a short and long menu. As Heaney says: *"The short gives guests an opportunity to come in and sample what we do, whereas the long tasting menu will give you the full experience.*

We also have Sunday roasts which are really popular."

"Personally I can get a bit bored of cooking a steak - as much as I enjoy it! Sometimes nothing beats a beautiful wild duck, pigeon or venison. Don't let it intimidate you, not only is it really accessible, it's also purse friendly, a lot leaner than most meats and tastes amazing."

Tommy Heaney

Chef Patron

www.heaneyscardiff.co.uk

6-10 Romilly Crescent
Pontcanna
Cardiff CF11 9NR
T: 02920 341264
E: info@heaneyscardiff.co.uk

HEANEYS

Ruth Hansom

Head Chef at The Princess of Shoreditch, London

"How are young chefs treating game? And what does the future look like for the future of game cookery? These are two really fascinating questions and no game guide should be complete without understanding what the future holds.

So, we talked to up and coming chef Ruth Hansom, the head chef of The Princess of Shoreditch and a contestant on Great British Menu in 2020. Ruth spent a number of years at The Ritz under John Williams who is, arguably, the leading game chef in the country.

"My earliest memory of game was while at The Ritz," she told us. "Chef (John Williams) made me try a game terrine while it was warm. I loved all the birds used in the terrine - pheasant, partridge, grouse any birds you can think of! It was magical cutting into the terrine once set and then tasting all of the different species of feathered game used - That is a memory that will stick with me forever."

A lot of younger chefs don't like game but this is probably more to do with unfamiliarity rather than taste. What is heartening about Ruth's memory of The Ritz is that when she had the opportunity to taste a dish as it was meant to be eaten she instantly responded.

"I love the seasonality," Ruth went on. "And I am excited by the different species available as the seasons change. I really like cooking parfaits and terrines. Game meat is also really nice pan-fried or confit - using any bits of carcass that you're not using on the plate for stocks and sauces.

"It is really important for people to keep using it and passing down the knowledge of how to use it, like John Williams did to me - This is when my own love affair with game began."

www.theprincessofshoreditch.com

James Martin Manchester

Restaurant

Greater Manchester

James Martin Manchester is run by well-known and much-loved celebrity chef James Martin and serves up classic, seasonally changing à la carte and special menus using exemplary local produce. Martin himself was a classically-trained chef and his vision is upheld by head chef Doug Crampton.

The restaurant is located in the historic Great Northern warehouse and the dining area sits beneath vaulted brick ceilings on a mezzanine within Manchester235 Casino. Imaginative original dishes feature seasonal ingredients from some of the UK's top meat, game, fish and cheese producers.

"British Game needs showcasing! We have a amazing larder of wild ingredients in the UK that so many people just don't know how to cook or what to do with. As chefs, we need to champion this amazing produce and celebrate it on our restaurant menus."

Doug Crampton
Head Chef

www.jamesmartinmanchester.co.uk

Manchester235
2 Watson Street
Manchester M3 4LP
T: 0161 828 0345
E: jamesmartin@manchester235.com

jamesMARTIN
MANCHESTER

Recipe

VENISON WELLINGTON

with New Potatoes and Buttered Baby Carrots

By Gary Maclean

This is a dish that I often do at home, the size of the loin makes it perfect for making a Wellington, it is very easy to pull together and can be done the day before.

Ingredients Serves 4

- 500g loin of venison
- 1 sheet butter puff pastry
- 1 pkt chestnut mushrooms
- 1 banana shallot
- 2 cloves
- Garlic
- 3 sprigs thyme, picked
- ¼ savoy cabbage
- 12 baby carrots
- 500g new potatoes
- 3 eggs
- 100g plain flour
- 50ml milk

Wine Pairing See page 165

Method

1. Firstly, season the loin of venison.
2. Heat the oil in a frying pan and sear the meat all over until you have achieved good colour on every surface of the meat.
3. Next get started on your mushroom mix, this is known as a duxelle, Melt the butter and soften the shallot and garlic.
4. Add the chopped mushrooms, herbs and seasoning, and cook until you have a paste-like mixture the time this takes depends on the moisture of the mushrooms.
5. Leave to cool.
6. Next blanch and refresh your cabbage leaves.
7. Your next task is to make a couple of French crepes, this is a very easy thing to make, take two eggs a splash of milk and a drop of oil whisk in enough flour until you get a thin batter consistency.
8. Taking a hot frying pan with a little oil pour a thin layer of the batter mix into the pan and swirl the pan until the mix creates a thin layer.
9. Cook the crepe out in the pan and turn over, repeat until you have two pancakes. For some reason the first one you make is never that good the second one is always better.
10. Overlap 2-3 sheets of cling film on a clean surface and lay the two crepes, slightly overlapping each one.
11. Taking some of your blanched cabbage leaves, dry them off using kitchen paper. Lay the cabbage onto the crepes.
12. Spread the cooled mushroom mixture all over the cabbage leaves, creating a thin, even layer.
13. Place the venison in the centre of the mushroom mixture. Using the edge of the cling film, carefully wrap the crepe, cabbage and mushroom mix around the fillet.
14. Roll into a sausage shape, twisting the ends of the cling film one side clockwise the other anticlockwise to form a tight log. Chill in the fridge for 30 minutes to firm up.
15. Meanwhile cook your potatoes and baby carrots.
16. On a lightly floured surface, place the pre-rolled puff pastry.
17. Unwrap your venison log and lay it in the middle of the pastry.
18. Fold over the bottom half of the pastry. Lightly brush the rest of the sheet with beaten egg.
19. Roll the whole thing around the meat to encase. Neatly trim the edges to create a parcel.
20. Transfer to a baking sheet and brush the pastry all over with beaten egg yolk.
21. Chill for at least 30 minutes.
22. Pre-heat your oven to 200°C
23. Using the back of a knife, mark the pastry, being careful not to cut all the way through.
24. Bake for 25 to 30 minutes.
25. Remove from oven and rest for 20 minutes.
26. Serve with your potatoes and vegetables.

Joshua Hunter at Holland & Holland

Restaurant

London

In the outskirts of north London, near Ruislip, you can find Holland & Holland's Shooting Grounds and within this complex there's a restaurant: Joshua Hunter at Holland and Holland.

Hunter learnt his trade working at top Michelin starred restaurants such as La Trompette, Murano and Kitchen W8.His focus is on using the very best of British produce sourced from the finest suppliers in the UK.

He has a love of fresh, seasonal and delicious food and his aim is to create mouth-watering menus that are quintessentially British, comforting and authentic.

"Holland & Holland is such a well know name within British shooting that it was always very important to me that we make game the centrepiece of the menus. Nothing makes me happier than hearing that someone has come in and tried grouse or partridge for the first time and really loved it."

Joshua Hunter

Head Chef

www.hollandandholland.com

Ducks Hill Road
Northwood
HA6 2ST
T: 01923 825349
E: shooting.grounds@hollandandholland.com

JOSHUA HUNTER at HOLLAND & HOLLAND SHOOTING GROUNDS

L'Ortolan

Restaurant

Berkshire

A string of well-known chefs have graced the kitchens at L'Ortolan over the years, all the way from Nico Ladenis in the 1980's through John Burton Race and on to Daniel Galmiche, Alan Murchison and then Tom Clarke.

The latest chef to head up the famous kitchen is James Greatorex and he continues the quest for excellence that his predecessors all strived for. L'Ortolan is set in a beautiful building near Reading in Berkshire in lovely surroundings and you can expect classical renditions of game all done with modern twists.

"Game is a key part of the menu at L'Ortolan. Autumn is my favourite season with bold earthy flavours and a vast array of fur and feathered game. It is also a nod to my background; growing up on the edge of the Peak District, local game was never far away and featured regularly on the family dinner table."

James Greatorex

Head Chef

MICHELIN STAR

www.lortolan.com

Church Lane
Shinfield
Reading RG2 9BY
T: 0118 9888500
E: info@lortolan.com

l'ortolan

La Trompette

Restaurant

London

La Trompette is a 1 Michelin star restaurant in Chiswick and is the sister restaurant of Chez Bruce. At the helm in the kitchen is Rob Weston who's career in fine dining is exemplary. Marco Pierre White, Guy Savoy in Paris and finally 15 years as Phil Howard's head chef at 2 star The Square.

Weston is a chef who likes to do things properly and game on the menu is a given. The menu changes twice a day and, according to Michelin the dishes on the menu are free of unnecessary adornment, so the focus remains on the top quality ingredients.

Rob Weston
Head Chef

Know your mushrooms

Craterellus cornucopioides, or horn of plenty, is an edible mushroom. It is also known as the black chanterelle, black trumpet, trompette de la mort (French), trombetta dei morti (Italian) or trumpet of the dead.

MICHELIN STAR

www.latrompette.co.uk

3-7 Devonshire Road
London
W4 2EU
T: 020 8747 1836
E: info@latrompette.co.uk

LA TROMPETTE

Lainston House

Hotel & Restaurant

Hampshire

Lainston House near Winchester in Hampshire is another of those gorgeous-looking properties that are so beloved of fans of the English country house. In the kitchen at Lainston is executive chef Phil Yeomans - a chef with a fine pedigree of experience and a lover of game.

Lainston House is food-focussed and uses ingredients from the kitchen garden and from the local area. Game is no exception to the menu in season with both rabbit and venison featuring on the a la carte.

"I love to cook game, its traditional and locally sourced from several shoots on our door step. Its so fresh and has great flavour. I use wild venison, partridge, pheasant, rabbit, grouse and pigeon;

I personally love partridge matched with butternut squash from our kitchen garden with a tradional bread sauce foam and elderberries which we pickle from the summer.

Our guests can enjoy a days shooting and bring the game back to the hotel where we prepare it for the evening and cook it for them, you don't get fresher than that!"

Phil Yeomans

Executive Chef

www.exclusive.co.uk/lainston-house/

Woodman Lane
Sparsholt
Winchester SO21 2LT
T: 01962 776088
E: www.exclusive.co.uk/lainston-house/

LAINSTON HOUSE

Le Gavroche

Restaurant

London

What is there to say about Le Gavroche that hasn't already been said? This stalwart institution of the London restaurant scene is the ultimate word in how to cook and serve game.

You'll find every conceivable type of game here from snipe and woodcock to deer and rabbit. Some of it will be carved at the table.

Michel Roux Jnr is one of the great chefs in the UK and his team, led by Rachel Humphrey, are game experts of the highest order. You'll also find a terrific wine list to enjoy with it.

"Game is part of Britain's food culture and history. We should recognise the real value of the game industry in providing quality food on a more sustainable basis. It's wonderful to present truly seasonal produce, for too many foods the seasons have disappeared, but game is very much the exception."

Michel Roux Jnr

Chef Patron

2 MICHELIN STAR

www.le-gavroche.co.uk

43 Upper Brook Street
London
W1K 7QR
T: 020 7408 0881 / 020 7499 1826
E: bookings@le-gavroche.co.uk

Le Manoir aux Quat'Saisons

Hotel & Restaurant

Oxfordshire

Another of the great restaurant institutions in the UK. Le Manoir, opened by Raymond Blanc in the 1980',s is still a byword for excellence and creativity.

There are few places that can match it for style and reputation and all of it is deserved, despite what you might have read - Jay Rayner once said it was the most expensive menu in Britain.

However, those that have had the opportunity to dine there speak of never-to-forget experiences and food to match.

"Wild Game is an essential part of our menu at Le Manoir. It captures the essence of the seasons and is a natural source of the British Larder."

Gary Jones
Executive Head Chef

2 MICHELIN STAR

www.belmond.com

Church Road
Great Milton
Oxford OX44 7PD
T: 01844 278881
E: manoir.mqs@belmond.com

LE MANOIR AUX QUAT'SAISONS
A BELMOND HOTEL
OXFORDSHIRE

Lewtrenchard Manor

Hotel & Restaurant

Devon

Nestled in a secluded valley beneath Dartmoor's wild tors, and virtually untouched by time, Lewtrenchard Manor is located in a magnificent setting. Steeped in history, this Jacobean manor dates back to the early 1600s and is the perfect place to enjoy a relaxing break, away from the modern world, in beautiful surroundings.

In the restaurant at Lewtrenchard, diners are treated to a dining experience that is without equal in the South West. Food is always meticulously prepared and beautifully presented by a team of talented chefs.

"We're are very lucky to have such a high quality aray of game in the South West.

We are situated on the edge of Dartmoor, so surrounded by a number of shoots which enables us to source game locally."

Duncan Murray
Owner

DOG FRIENDLY

www.lewtrenchard.co.uk

Lewtrenchard
Okehampton
Devon EX20 4PN
T: 01566 783222
E: info@lewtrenchard.co.uk

LEWTRENCHARD MANOR

Loyton Lodge

Restaurant

Devon

Since joining Loyton Lodge in August 2017, chef Adam Fanson has quickly made the Kitchen at Loyton his own. The Kitchen provides guests with bespoke menus worked from exceptional ingredients from their own farm, walled kitchen garden and the local area.

Seasonality is uppermost and Adam takes direct inspiration from what is available - wild garlic when it arrives along the streams will be incorporated into the menu along with game - the most sustainable product of the estate. Everything gets used including hedgerow berries in puddings and liqueurs.

Adam Fanson
Executive Chef

Did you know?

One of the shoots managed by Loyton is at Combe Sydenham which was once home to Sir Francis Drake, the famous Elizabethan sea captain. Drake was also a skilled water engineer and a series of leats and ponds at the centre of the shoot can still be seen.

www.loyton.com

Loyton Estate
Morebath
Tiverton
Devon EX16 9AS
T: 01398 331 051 E: thelodge@loyton.com

LOYTON LODGE

Lucknam Park

Hotel, Restaurant & Spa

Wiltshire

Hywel Jones has been executive chef at Lucknam Park, near Chippenham in Wiltshire for over 15 years and has built a solid fine-dining culture within the hotel and the restaurant: Restaurant Hywel Jones.

His background of working for both Marco Pierre White and Nico Ladenis shows in the way the dishes are constructed and Lucknam is ideally situated to take advantage of stunning local ingredients which also come from Jones's native Wales. The hotel features a well known spa and brasserie and is set in its own, impressive grounds, the tree-lined drive being a highlight.

Hywel Jones
Executive Chef

Did you know?

Lucknam Park has a splendid mile-long drive lined with 400 lime and beech trees. During World War II Spitfire and Hurricane planes from a local airfield were hidden along its length. The huge trees provided perfect camouflage.

MICHELIN STAR

www.lucknampark.co.uk

Colerne
Chippenham
Wiltshire SN14 8AZ
T: 01225 742777
E: enquiries@lucknampark.co.uk

1720
LUCKNAM PARK
HOTEL | SPA | ESTATE

Mere

Restaurant

London

Mere, located in Fitzrovia in London, is not an obvious choice of restaurant for this guide. But on deciding on entries we felt it was important to include places that were not run-of-the-mill. Mere is run by Monica Galetti and her husband David. Monica is better known as one of the presenters of Masterchef: The Professionals.

Her background at Le Gavroche along with her Samoan roots give Mere an edge of creativity and classicalism that is instantly appealing. Game is treated with care but with unusual interpretations at this modern classic.

"Game is an amazing product and the season is one to which we always look forward.

It is something very special here in the UK and there's a huge variety in terms of what you can get, the flavours are fantastic."

Monica Galetti
Chef Patron

www.mere-restaurant.com

74 Charlotte Stree
London
W1T 4QH
T: 0207 268 6565
E: bookings@mere-restaurant.com

MERE

Midsummer House

Restaurant

Cambridgeshire

Daniel Clifford's Cambridge restaurant has continued to climb the culinary ladder since he took over as head chef in 1998. In 2002 he won a Michelin Star and in 2005 added another. Since then, Midsummer House has continued to grow in reputation and culinary ability.

Located on the banks of The River Cam next to Midsummer Common the restaurant is both classical and modern with a firm foundation. Game, when it is on the menu, is treated with the respect it deserves and harmonised into overall menus where it often takes pride of place.

Daniel Clifford

Chef Patron

Did you know?

Midsummer House has been a private residence for most of its life, as well as a dog breeding home and lodgings for the public house next door. It first got turned into a restaurant in the 1980s when it was bought by Food & Drink's Chris Kelly.

2 MICHELIN STAR

midsummerhouse.co.uk

Midsummer Common
Cambridge
CB4 1HA
T: 01223 369299
E: reservations@midsummerhouse.co.uk

Midsummer House

Moor Hall

Restaurant with Rooms

Lancashire

Moor Hall is a fine dining restaurant where you'll find a tasting menu concept featuring exact flavour combinations and perfectly presented dishes. Game, when it is on the menu, will be exciting and paired with ingredients that may take you by surprise.

Chef Patron Mark Birchall was head chef at Simon Rogan's 2 star restaurant L'Enclume and now has 2 stars of his own at Moor Hall near Ormskirk which was recently voted best restaurant in the UK.

Mark Birchall is, unquestionably, one of the UK's finest chefs.

"We want to celebrate the amazing game we have in the UK. Serving wild but sustainable game is key to our ethos".

Mark Birchall
Chef Patron

2 MICHELIN STAR

www.moorhall.com

Prescot Road
Aughton
Lancashire L39 6RT
T: 01695 572511
E: enquiry@moorhall.com

MOOR HALL
RESTAURANT WITH ROOMS

Morston Hall

Hotel & Restaurant

Norfolk

Morston is the Norfolk home of much loved chef Galton Blackiston. Game plays a big part of kitchen life at Morston Hall as Galton is a lover of hunting and shooting on the local marshlands.

Morston offers a set 8 courses designed to be a balanced collection of tastes and flavours. In season you'll find every type of game on the menu with pairings suited to the unique flavours of each bird or species.

Ducks are a favourite but expect luxurious cooking techniques and classical accompaniments to play a part of the evening.

"Game has always featured heavily during the season on my menus. We use the full spectrum starting from grouse on the glorious 12 to hare, teal and wild mallard you name it, we use it.

It's lean, sustainable, seasonal and above all very tasty so it makes sense"

Galton Blackiston
Chef Patron

MICHELIN STAR

DOG FRIENDLY

www.morstonhall.com

The Street
Morston
Norfolk NR25 7AA
T: 01263 741041
E: reception@morstonhall.com

morstonhall

Northcote Manor

Hotel & Restaurant

Lancashire

Northcote Manor has been at the pinnacle of Lancashire dining since the early 1990's when co-founder Nigel Haworth was at the stoves. Today, the kitchens are under the eagle eye of TV favourite Lisa Goodwin-Allen. She draws her inspiration from the beautiful Ribble Valley landscape and the rich bounty that the region has to offer.

Game is a favourite. Lisa grew up with game birds that her dad would bring home and her grandmother would cook. *"It's about taking that local produce and putting my twist on it,"* she says.

"What I love about game is its versatility. You really can take in any direction you want. Of course, there are classic, time-honoured recipes and I love them. But sometimes when you go out to dinner at somewhere like Northcote you are looking for a new experience and that's what we do."

Lisa Goodwin-Allen
Executive Chef

MICHELIN STAR

www.northcote.com

Langho
Blackburn
Lancashire BB6 8BE
T: 01254 240 555
E: reception@northcote.com

northcote
A STAFFORD COLLECTION HOTEL

Galton Blackiston

Morston Hall, Norfolk

" Game is all about the seasons.

Galton Blackiston, owner of Morston Hall in Norfolk, has had game on his menu for as long as he can remember. To him every type of game has a role to play and a place on his menu.

"It's all about the seasons," he told The Great Game Guide. "I'm passionate about field sports and I love shooting but what I shoot must end up in the pot at the end of the day.

"At Morston Hall we have a slightly unusual set-up. We only do 50 covers a night and that is made up of a set menu of eight courses. I wouldn't call it a tasting menu. From the first day of the grouse season to the last day of shooting in January we have piece of game on the menu as part of the set offer.

"I love grouse, partridge, pheasant, hare and teal. They are all persona favourites though I think the teal is my absolute favourite. It's a small duck but its highly flavoured and the taste can really depend on where the birds have been feeding. We're on the coast here in Norfolk which is marshy and wet and very well suited to ducks.

"Basically, throughout the season whatever I get offered in the way of game I invariably use it but what we do on the menu is different to what I do at home. To me roast pheasant for Sunday lunch is my all time favourite. I served it the old-fashioned way with bread sauce and bacon. It's truly delicious.

"But in the restaurant we'd do it a little more luxuriously. Probably a ballotine cooked in the water bath (because game has a tendency to be dry if you're not careful.) We will invariably use some foie gras or truffle and make an amazing sauce from the bones.

"Game is a celebration of seasonality. It challenges us in the kitchen and inspires us to do it justice."

MH morstonhall

www.morstonhall.com

One Aldwych

Hotel & Restaurant

London

Chef Dominic Teague and One Aldwych is one of London's best kept chef secrets. A truly dedicated chef who trained with Jeff Galvin at Soho's famous L'Escargot restaurant, among others.

His skills are evident in every dish where simple cooking techniques are paired with outstanding sourcing of ingredients.

It takes bravery and courage to remove everything from a dish that doesn't need to be there and when game is on the menu you can expect clean, well-cooked and perfectly judged renditions of classic flavours.

"For me, game is right up there with the best of British produce. It has wonderfully versatility, great nutritional content, generally good value and is a challenge to cook properly. We are so lucky to have such variety and quality on our doorstop and eagerly look forward to the glorious twelfth each year!"

Dominic Teague
Executive Chef

www.onealdwych.com

1 Aldwych
London
WC2B 4BZ
T: 0207 300 1000
E: reservations@onealdwych.com

ONEALDWYCH

Interview

Cyrus Todiwala

Cafe Spice Namasté, London

Chef Cyrus Todiwala has been at the forefront of Asian cuisine for over 25 years with his restaurant Cafe Spice Namasté regularly on top lists of eating out destinations. His thoughts on game are revolutionary and not for the reasons you might think. The Great Game Guide editor Chandos Elletson asked him what it is about game that keeps him coming back for more.

"You have to remember one simple things about game in India," Cyrus began. "It wasn't that long ago that animals were domesticated in India. Before that everything was hunted. That means that we have been working out how to cook game and preserve it for thousands of years. And the way we do it is very different to the way it is done over here - because it is hotter in India.

"My father hunted for everything. In that I was lucky to have access to many different species and flavours growing up. One of the first things I did when I opened my first restaurant was to get hold of some wild boar and pickle it.

"You shouldn't find that surprising. Pickling is the way we preserve meat in India. In Europe the art of drying has been commonplace and that's due to the climate as much as anything. In India it can be too hot to air dry. So, we developed the art of pickling.

"But, don't be fooled by common restaurant practice where guests eat papadums with spoonful's of pickles as a starter. What I mean by pickles is

how an Indian at home would eat it. We have a fairly bland meal of lentil dhal and rice and on the side we add a pickle. This can be a meat pickle or vegetable pickle. Game makes amazing pickles. My Rajastahni venison pickle is flavoured with nigella seeds and browned onions and makes a superb accompaniment".

www.cafespice.co.uk

CAFÉ SPICE NAMASTÉ

Recipe

Wine
Pairing
See page
165
the great game guide
2021/22
PURNELL'S

Pheasant 'Maryland'

by Glynn Purnell

Chef Patron at Purnell's Restaurant

Retro! Retro! Read all about it! This garnish is to cooking what flares and sideburns are to fashion. When people see this recipe, they'll probably think I've lost the plot, but it's proper sick! It works and it's great fun, and if you're up for deep frying the banana with the skin on (make sure it's kept out of the fridge and is really dry), you'll get a delicious, rich and buttery banana.

Banana, sweetcorn fritters and lightly spiced pot-roasted pheasant - it's a 70's classic from a 70's child. It's flares, it's disco and best of all, it's delicious.

Ingredients Serves 4

PHEASANT

- 1 teaspoon smoked paprika
- 1 teaspoon cajun spice mix
- 1 teaspoon ground ginger
- 2 pheasants, crown only with wishbone removed
- Splash of vegetable oil
- 1 carrot, peeled and chopped
- 1 celery stick
- 1 onion, peeled and chopped
- Garlic clove, peeled
- 75ml brandy
- 200ml hot chicken stock
- Knob of butter
- Splash of double cream

SWEETCORN FRITTERS

- 100g self-raising flour
- 1 large freerange egg
- 3 tablespoons stout
- 195g can of sweetcorn, drained
- 2 spring onions, thinly sliced
- ½ bunch chives, chopped
- Salt
- Ground ginger, to taste
- Vegetable oil for deep frying

BANANAS

- 2 ripe bananas in their skins, at room temperature

Method

PHEASANT

1. Preheat the oven to 170°c/gas mark 3.
2. Mix the paprika, Cajun spice mix and ginger together and rub the mixture all over the pheasants.
3. Heat a little vegetable oil in a flameproof casserole dish and brown the pheasants on all sides. Remove from dish and set aside.
4. Add the carrot, celery, onion, and garlic to the dish and cook until lightly coloured, then return the pheasants to the dish.
5. Pour the brandy over the pheasants and set the alcohol alight, then add the stock. Put the lid on the dish and transfer to the onion for 12-15 minutes.
6. Lift the pheasants out of the dish and leave to rest in a warm place. Pour the liquor into a saucepan and simmer over a medium heat until reduced by half. Keep warm.

SWEETCORN FRITTERS

1. Put the flour in a bowl and make a well in the centre. Beat the egg with the beer and add to the well. Gradually beat the flour into the liquid to make a smooth batter, then stir in the sweetcorn, spring onions and chives. Season to taste with salt and ginger.
2. Heat the vegetable oil in a deep-fat fryer or deep saucepan until it reaches 180°c.
3. Drop large spoonfuls of the fritter mixture into the hot oil and deep-fry for about 3 minutes until golden brown all over. Drain from the oil and keep warm.

BANANAS

1. Remove any moisture from the outside of the bananas and deep-fry in the fritter oil at 180°c for about 3 minutes until the skin is golden brown. Drain from the oil, pat dry and cut in half lengthways.

TO FINISH

1. Remove the pheasant breast meat from the bone. Add the knob of butter and splash of cream to the sauce and stir well.
2. Place the meat on serving plates with a fritter and a piece of deep-fried banana. Drizzle with the sauce.

Parlour

Pub & Restaurant

London

Jesse Dunford Wood is a maverick chef who never does anything the way you expect and that's what makes his Parlour restaurant, in Kensal Green, London, so exciting and so different.

It says this on the website: funky salads, kyivs and cow pies, soufflés and rolos - what's your favourite?

You don't really need to know much more other than when game is on the menu it will be surprising and done in a way that might not be quite what you were expecting. But that's the beauty of eating out!

"I love game because of the unexpected nature of the wild British seasonal larder that affords us the finest array of native species.

Some might be scared by deep strong flavours, but there really is something for everyone at every level!"

Jesse Dunford Wood
Chef Patron

www.parlourkensal.com

5 Regent Street
Kensal Green
London NW10 5LG
T: 020 8969 2184
E: hello@parlourkensal.com

Pashcoe House

Restaurant with Rooms

Devon

If you're into shooting then you will love Devon's Pashcoe House where you can combine clay shooting with country house dining all wrapped up in The South West's best small hotel of the year.

Set in twenty-five acres of wild Devon landscapes overlooking a lake with rolling fields in all directions, Paschoe House is an idyllic oasis. In the kitchen head chef James Checkley is passionate about creating exciting dishes from local and sustainably sourced ingredients, including game. The restaurant is also a showcase for home-grown ingredients from the walled garden.

"The start of game season is an exciting time for all chefs. At Paschoe House we always get excited to start using game, taking us into autumn. The flavour and variety that is available from game makes it a truly special season. From venison to pheasant we constantly use the best Devon game on our menus."

James Checkley
Head Chef

Photo credit: © Matt Austin

DOG FRIENDLY

www.paschoehouse.co.uk

Bow
Crediton
Devon EX17 6JT
T: 01363 84244
E: theteam@paschoehouse.co.uk

PASCHOE HOUSE
DEVON

Paul Ainsworth at No6

Restaurant

Cornwall

Paul Ainsworth is the definition of a hard-working chef who trained in top kitchens and is now enjoying the fruits of his labour. His restaurant, Paul Ainsworth at No6, is justly famous in Cornwall and beyond and for good reason. Paul trained under Gary Rhodes, Gordon Ramsay and Marcus Wareing and their discipline and eye for detail are hallmarks of the Ainsworth style.

Along with his wife Emma Paul now runs a handful of excellent eateries around Padstow and Rock. When it's on the menu game will be perfect.

"Game is one of our favourite meats to serve to our guests at our restaurants. It's a really healthy addition to our diets, being leaner and lower in cholesterol compared to pork or lamb, as well as incredibly tasty.

On the taster menu at Mahé's Chef Table experience, which is our development kitchen at Paul Ainsworth at No6, we have Trefranck Farm's beautiful organically-farmed Red Deer taking centre stage. One of our most popular game recipes is our roast grouse with bread sauce and crispy homemade chips."

Paul Ainsworth
Chef Patron

MICHELIN STAR

www.paul-ainsworth.co.uk

6 Middle Street
Padstow
Cornwall PL28 8AP
T: 01841 532093
E: info@paul-ainsworth.co.uk

Paul Ainsworth at no 6

Pipe & Glass

Pub & Restaurant

Yorkshire

Situated on the edge of the Dalton estate in East Yorkshire, the Pipe and Glass is a former coaching inn, with parts of the building dating back to the 17th century. In 2006.

James and Kate Mackenzie took over the Pipe and Glass and have created a warm, comfortable Yorkshire country pub, where customers can drop in for a pint of local ale, tuck into classic 'pub grub' dishes or enjoy the highest standards of modern cuisine.

James' menus represent his signature style of imaginative British cooking, using as much high quality local and seasonal produce as possible.

"When you are situated rurally, as we are at the Pipe and Glass, it's hard not to love game, not only is it part of the tradition and heritage of our local area but game is lean, sustainable meat with delicious flavour. Game features on the menu at the Pipe and Glass all year round as it is always hugely popular with our customers."

James Mackenzie
Chef Patron

Photo credit: © Tim Green

MICHELIN STAR

www.pipeandglass.co.uk

West End
South Dalton
East Yorkshire HU17 7PN
T: 01430 810246
E: email@pipeandglass.co.uk

pipe and glass

Pollen Street Social

Restaurant

London

Jason Atherton is a rare chef and his ability to stay under the radar so he can focus on running outstanding restaurants is a credit to him and his team. Make no mistake, Jason Atherton is exquisitely talented and one of a number of chefs to come through the Gordon Ramsay school of excellence.

Pollen Street Social is a classic London restaurant that highlights Atherton's skill: an ability to pare down dishes until they are perfect in every way. The restaurant received a star after six months in 2011. It's not hard to see why.

Jason Atherton
Chef Patron

The Jason Empire

Jason Atherton has become a truly international chef with restaurants all over the world. You can find his footprint in London, Shanghai, Dubai, St Moritz and New York. His latest venture is in Harrods.

MICHELIN STAR

www.pollenstreetsocial.com

8-10 Pollen Street
Mayfair
London W1S 1NQ
T: +44 20 7290 7600
E: reservations@pollenstreetsocial.com

POLLEN STREET SOCIaL JASON ATHERTON

Princess of Shoreditch

Restaurant

London

With new addition Ruth Hansom in the kitchen The Princess takes its food up a gear and offers a seasonal menu changing throughout the year. The ground floor bar serves a bar menu paired with a fantastic selection of wines, craft beers, ales and carefully curated cocktails, whilst upstairs has a completely new feel focused on British provenance. Game is treated the way it ought to be as Ruth trained under John Williams at The Ritz. "I love the seasonality of game," she told us. "And I am excited by the different species available as the seasons change."

"Game is readily available, delicious and seasonal. Although not unique to the UK, the UK is widely famed for it.

I love the seasonality of game meat and plan my menu around it."

Ruth Hansom
Head Chef

www.theprincessofshoreditch.com

76-78 Paul Street
London
EC2A 4NE
T: 020 7729 9270
E: info@theprincessofshoreditch.com

The Princess OF SHOREDITCH

Purnell's

Restaurant

West Midlands

Raised in Birmingham, a multicultural and exciting city, Glynn Purnell brings a love of game to his Michelin starred restaurant. Guests can expect the unexpected from this popular chef and regular star on TV.

As Glynn says himself in the foreword to this guide: "A curveball of cooking has emerged on my menus. My take on venison is now with an orange, sichuan and ponzu gel; I do a radical duck with almond satay and a crazy Pheasant Maryland with - yes, rub your eyes - a banana.

And that's how exciting game can be."

"When cooking game, a lot of cooks and chefs will always turn to the classic and traditional methods of preparing and serving. The likes of venison with Grand Veneur sauce, mallard with orange, and pheasant or partridge served with game crisps and bread sauce are all traditional and delicious dishes. But as the UK has become more diverse, it has put a whole new perspective on what I choose to serve with game."

Glynn Purnell - Chef Patron

MICHELIN STAR

www.purnellsrestaurant.com

55 Cornwall Street
Birmingham
B3 2DH
T: 0121 212 9799
E: info@purnellsrestaurant.com

PURNELL'S

Quo Vadis

Restaurant

London

Jeremy Lee is a classic cook and has been for a very long time. His style is similar to chefs Simon Hopkinson and Alastair Little with whom he worked.

He has found a home and a restaurant now that suits his vision and his food and that place is Quo Vadis on Dean Street in Soho. It's a classic building in a classic location and like many of the entries in this guide there are certain places that simply have to be included.

Tan leather booths, panelled wood flooring and stained-glass windows are the backdrop for a seasonal menu that has plenty of game done properly.

"The food of the wilds is vital to the kitchen. As the calendar wends its way through the year, we delight in dishes on the menu that rejoice in the lean flavoursome meat of venison, the depth of flavour of hare, not to mention the terrines made from wild rabbit. The bones from game, both furred and feathered make stock as distinctive as the meat - making for wonderful pies. There is a shout of great joy when the game season for birds begins in August, with the first grouse swiftly followed by grey leg partridge. And as the year draws to a close, woodcock and snipe take pride of place before the wild ducks of winter bolster us with marvellous meat that delight in the preserves made from autumn fruits."

Jeremy Lee
Chef Patron

www.quovadissoho.co.uk

26-29 Dean Street
Soho
London W1D 3LL
T: 0207 437 9585
E: reception@quovadissoho.co.uk

quo vadis

Restaurant Andrew Fairlie

Restaurant

Perth and Kinross

Game is taken very seriously at Restaurant Andrew Fairlie. Chef Stevie McLaughlin took over the running of the restaurant following the death of Andrew Fairlie in early 2019.

Restaurant Andrew Fairlie is Scotland's only 2 star restaurant and one of the best restaurants in the UK. It is located within Gleneagles Hotel but operated independently.

A strong team in both kitchen and front of house ensure classical standards laid down by Andrew Fairlie are continued.

As a prime seasonal ingredient you can expect game dishes to be well thought out and expertly presented.

2 MICHELIN STAR

"Scottish game in season will always feature on our menus at Restaurant Andrew Fairlie. My love and admiration for Scottish game comes from the fact that it can only be handled at specific times each year. This helps ensure that the ingredients we are working with are in their absolute peak condition.

Stevie McLaughlin
Head Chef

www.andrewfairle.co.uk

Gleneagles Hotel
Auchterarder
PH3 1NF Scotland
T: 01764 694267
E: reservations@andrewfairlie.co.uk

Restaurant Martin Wishart

Restaurant

Edinburgh

Martin Wishart is a classically trained chef who worked in London under Albert Roux, Marco Pierre White and others. His beautiful waterside restaurant is located on The Water of Leith just north of Edinburgh in the old docks and is a must-visit for game lovers in season.

When he was working in London he was always proud to see Scottish ingredients like game and shellfish on the menus. But now, with all that Scotland has to offer on his doorstep, he feels fortunate to get them even fresher.

Martin Wishart
Chef Patron

Historic Leith

The district of Leith rests on the shores of the Firth of Forth, at the mouth of the Water of Leith. Having served as the port of Edinburgh for hundreds of years, the area's original harbour dates back to the 14th century and has been visited by many travelling kings and queens, including Mary Queen of Scots and King George IV.

MICHELIN STAR

www.restaurantmartinwishart.co.uk

54 The Shore
Leith
Edinburgh EH6 6RA
T: 0131 553 3557
E: info@martin-wishart.co.uk

RESTAURANT MARTIN WISHART

Half Roasted Partridge

with White Bean, Wild Mushrooms, Herb Oil, Thyme & Garlic

By Ian Gibbs, Head Chef at The East End Arms

Ingredients Serves 2

- 1 whole partridge
- 100g cooked white beans
- 50g butter
- 100g wild mushrooms (prepared and sliced)
- 50ml dry sherry
- 75ml double cream
- 100ml veal jus (or good base gravy)
- 1tsp truffle oil
- 2 finely diced shallots
- 6 unpeeled garlic cloves (2 cloves peeled and crushed)
- 1 bunch thyme
- 100g rainbow chard or cavolo nero (lightly blanched)
- 50ml pre-prepared parsley oil
- Vegetable oil
- Sea salt & black pepper

Method

1. On the stove heat a pan, add the oil, season and sear the partridge ensuring an even caramelisation of the skin. Add the garlic cloves and 6 sprigs of thyme.
2. Transfer to the oven, 190˚c or gas mark 5, for 12-16 minutes or probe to 63˚c. When cooked, rest for 15 minutes.
3. Whilst the partridge is roasting warm the veal jus and set aside.
4. In a second pan add butter, shallots and crushed garlic. Sauté for 2 minutes, then add the wild mushrooms. Cook until the mushrooms are soft then deglaze the pan with the sherry, flambé and reduce by half.
5. Add the white beans and double cream and 1 tablespoon of the veal jus for flavour. Slowly reduce to a binding consistency, set aside and keep warm. Finally, add the beans and truffle oil. Season to taste.
6. Warm the blanched rainbow chard or cavolo nero in foaming butter and drain on kitchen paper.
7. To plate, place the beans centrally in a large bowl, arrange the greens on the bean mix.
8. Split the partridge carefully in half removing the rib cage bones and place the meat gently on top of the vegetables.
9. Add the roasted garlic cloves and thyme, then dress the plate with the veal jus and parsley oil.

Wine Pairing
See page 165

Restaurant Sat Bains

Restaurant with Rooms

Nottinghamshire

In many ways Sat Bains exemplifies the excitement currently running through British cooking. His heritage, his methods and his energy all contribute to a menu style that is completely unique.

Under Sat Bains' care an evening of gastronomy takes a leap off a cliff but as each course follows another a realisation dawns: a parachute of flavours, ideas and textures brings you softly down to earth. With 2 Michelin Stars and an army of fans the future of restaurants is ensured because this is creative cooking at its finest.

"Game is a way of life in British culture and as a chef it is essential to work with the seasons. Game season, for me, is one of the most exciting as tasting food at its wildest from the best ethical suppliers is what its all about. All chefs should have game on their menus in season. It is delicious and super seasonal."

Sat Bains
Chef Patron

2 MICHELIN STAR

www.restaurantsatbains.com

Lenton Lane
Nottingham
NG7 2SA
T: 0115 986 6566
E: info@rsb.uk.com

rsb

Rules

Restaurant

London

The oldest restaurant in London is also, remarkably, one of it's best kept secrets. Rules continues, year after year, doing the same thing it has always done: serve wonderful, traditional French/ English food in an atmosphere like no other. And that is the secret of its longevity. It knows its strengths.

Rules is cosy, elegant and with decor from another time but don't be fooled: dinner at Rules will linger long in the memory especially if game is involved and it is plentiful on the menu from game soup to young grouse.

David Stafford
Head Chef

Literary heaven

Many famous writers have loved Rules over the centuries including several who have mentioned the restaurant in their stories. Most notably Graham Greene in The End of the Affair. Dickens was a regular and Evelyn Waugh loved it.

www.rules.co.uk

35 Maiden Lane
Covent Garden
London WC2E 7LB
T: 020 7836 5314
E: info@rules.co.uk

Simpsons

Restaurant

East Midlands

Edgbaston may be famous for the cricket but in restaurant terms it only means one place: Simpsons - one of Birmingham's most loved restaurants and owned by chef Andreas Antona with chef director Luke Tipping in charge of the kitchens.

The restaurant has held a star for many years and a recent redesign has transformed the dining space into a bright, modern restaurant inspired by the colours and shapes of nature. Simpsons is all tasting menu now but a dedication to seasonality means that game gets a good showing.

Luke Tipping

Executive Chef

Did you know?

In the 19th century, Edgbaston was under the control of the Gough-Calthorpe and Gillott families. They refused to allow factories or warehouses to be built thus making it attractive for the wealthier residents of Birmingham. It then came to be known as *"where the trees begin"*.

MICHELIN STAR

www.simpsonsrestaurant.co.uk

20 Highfield Road
Edgbaston
Birmingham B15 3DU
T: 0121 4543434
E: info@simpsonsrestaurant.co.uk

SIMPSONS

Skosh

Restaurant

Yorkshire

Chef Neil Bentinck opened Skosh in York in 2016 as a bespoke dining room with an open kitchen to offer uncomplicated, yet refined dishes. Located in a Grade II listed building just beyond the Micklegate bar in the historic city centre the menu revolves around the idea of snacking with small plates.

However, the feel of the cooking at Skosh is definitely towards Asian trends as several recent menu items indicated: Thai-style venison sausage, venison tataki, pheasant yakitori. It's exciting to see chefs approaching game from new angles and not being afraid to experiment with new flavours and techniques.

"I am a huge fan of using game on the menu and it's always an exciting time of the year when the produce starts to arrive in the kitchen!

Firstly, game meat is so full of flavour and really delicious but just as importantly is its provenance. The direct benefit is keeping trade within the community. It is local, seasonal produce and it really drives our menus at skosh. So much of the game we work with goes beautifully with big, bold & spicy flavours."

Neil Bentinck
Chef Patron

www.skoshyork.co.uk

98 Micklegate
York
YO1 6JX
T: 01904 634849
E: info@skoshyork.co.uk

skosh.

Sorrel

Restaurant

Surrey

Chef Steve Drake's pioneering approach to gastronomy is finally blossoming at his Dorking restaurant, Sorrel. His training was Nico and Marco but his style is pure Marc Veyrat of L'Auberge de l'Eridan in Annecy where he trained after winning The Roux Scholarship in 2001.

Steve Drake's obsession is flavour combinations and his menu is filled with ideas and insights into finding just the right partner flavour for any ingredient.

At Sorrel this can result in unexpected twists. When it's on the menu game will be sure to surprise.

Photo credit: © Paul Judd

Steve Drake

Chef Patron

Did you know?

Sorrel herb plants are small edible green leafed plants related to rhubarb and buckwheat. There are three main varieties: broad leaf, French (buckler leaf), and red-veined sorrel.

MICHELIN STAR

www.sorrelrestaurant.co.uk

77 South Street
Dorking
Surrey RH4 2JU
T: 01306 889414
E: info@sorrelrestaurant.co.uk

SORREL

St John

Restaurant

London

There is no more iconic restaurant than St John and no other chef like Fergus Henderson. The St John style has been endlessly copied and reworked in other kitchens but there is nothing like the original. Nose to tail eating suits game so well and over the years many exceptional game dishes have come and gone.

What you'll find on the menu when you visit is hard to tell but whatever it is it will be memorable and stamped with authenticity. Just to read about dishes such as Pheasant Pie is enough to get most guests into a taxi and off to Smithfield.

Fergus Henderson

Chef Patron

Did you know?

St John was opened in 1994 by Trevor Gulliver, Jon Spiteri and Fergus Henderson in a former bacon smoke-house close to the old Smithfield meat market. However, it had also been a greenhouse, beer store and a squat.

MICHELIN STAR

www.stjohnrestaurant.com

26 St. John Street
London
EC1M 4AY
T: 020 7251 0848
E: info@stjohnrestaurant.com

St. JOHN

The Angel at Hetton

Restaurant with Rooms

Yorkshire

One of the great old pubs of northern England has had a transformation with the arrival of vastly experienced chef Michael Wignall and his wife Joanne.

The Angel at Hetton is now firmly back on the gastronomic map with Wignall, who held 2 Michelin stars at his previous restaurant at Pennyhill Park, a determined game lover.

He to told us how important game is to a rural community and that it is always on the menu as long as it is available - and that it is a real highlight.

"Game shooting and eating is at the heart of most rural communities in the UK and it's important that we keep the tradition going. Being a chef in the heart of the Yorkshire Dales it's important to work with the season and game is a real highlight, I have it on the menu for as long as

I can. It's versatile, readily available and, of course, the flavour is second to none."

Michael Wignall
Chef Patron

MICHELIN STAR

www.angelhetton.co.uk

Hetton
Skipton
BD23 6LT
T: 01756 730263
E: reservations@angelhetton.co.uk

THE ANGEL
AT HETTON

The Beach House

Restaurant

Glamorgan

There's a lot to love about The Beach House: A Michelin star, it's superb position right on the sands of Oxwich Bay and a really good chef in Hywel Griffith.

The food is focussed on the seasonal and local but sharpened by Griffith's love of game and hunting and his experience in kitchens like The Chester Grosvenor, Ynyshir Hall and, finally, as head chef at The Freemasons at Wiswell (see separate listings). Game is a passion and features all season in various guises and across the range of game birds and animals.

"Game to me is a fantastic, diverse and sustainable British product from partridge, rabbits and grouse all the way up to the largest wild mammal we have in the UK: the red deer. To me as a chef it's important to follow the seasons as that's when produce is at its best."

Hywel Griffith
Chef Patron

MICHELIN STAR

www.beachhouseoxwich.co.uk

Oxwich Beach
Gower
Swansea SA3 1LS
T: 01792 390965
E: reservations@beachhouseoxwich.co.uk

BEACH HOUSE
RESTAURANT

The Beacon

Pub & Restaurant

Kent

Set in gorgeous countryside with stunning views The Beacon is located in Tea Garden Lane, Tonbridge Wells and is a restaurant concept by Scott Goss and partner Peter Cornwell. It's been described as a naturally abundant and delicious home for caring, sharing and giving.

The restaurant, private dining, bar, and terrace is set in seventeen acres with three lakes. The Beacon kitchen team pick and get inspiration from the natural surroundings and bring a fresh menu every season.

"Being in the Kent Countryside we are surrounded by the very best game. Game season is a very special time of year - a time of year chefs get super creative and a time to reflect on brilliant timeless classics."

Scott Goss
Executive Chef

www.illbemother.co.uk/thebeacon

Tea Garden Lane
Royal Tunbridge Wells
Kent TN3 9JH
T: 01892 524252
E: hello@the-beacon.co.uk

THE BEACON
GARDEN KITCHEN

The Bell Inn

Pub & Restaurant

Gloucestershire

There are some pubs that just exude appeal and The Bell Inn in Langford is one of them. It's run by Peter Creed and Tom Noest and focuses on good simple pub food with a straightforward wine list, spirits and beer selection.

There's a cosy bar area with lots of seating, a separate restaurant with open fire and also a large beer garden with countryside view.

With plenty of interesting game on the menu this could be that holy grail pub that all game enthusiasts should head for.

Tom Noest
Chef Patron

Did you know?

The beautiful Grade 1 listed church of St Matthew in Langford has a ring of six bells. Four were cast in 1741. The tenor and treble bells were cast by the Whitechapel Bell Foundry in 1953.

www.thebelllangford.com

Langford
Nr Burford
Gloucestershire GL7 3LF
T: 01367 860249
E: info@thebelllangford.com

THE BELL INN
LANGFORD

The Black Bull Sedbergh

Restaurant

Cumbria

Formerly a 17th century coaching inn, which has been lovingly and sympathetically restored. A great deal of care and attention has gone into creating unique and distinctive spaces...

Owned and run by husband and wife team James Ratcliffe and Nina Matsunaga, The Black Bull in Sedburgh is a pub with a difference. Head chef Nina was born in Germany to Japanese parents and brings a deep knowledge of baking and game cookery to the menu.

The Black Bull is all about local meat, local vegetables and local game and you can expect to find very modern and alternative interpretations on the menu alongside the classics. Situated on the edge of The Lake District this should be a destination of choice.

"The Black Bull's restaurant is very much focused on serving a true field to fork menu. Our food ethos is simple and that is to use only the best seasonal ingredients available from the ever-changing larder on our doorstep and that includes a wide variety of British seasonal game."

Nina Matsunaga
Chef Patron

www.theblackbullsedbergh.co.uk

44 Main Street
Sedbergh
Cumbria LA10 5BL
T: 015396 20264
E: bookings@theblackbullsedbergh.co.uk

The Black Swan at Oldstead

Restaurant with Rooms

North Yorkshire

There's something magical about The Black Swan. For starters it's hard to find and when you get there it appears to be a regular old pub. But appearances can be deceptive. Inside is a chef of real skill, Tommy Banks, who grew up on a nearby farm, doesn't have a long list of previous experience and yet turns out some of the best food in the UK - much of it grown on the premises.

What isn't farmed is properly sourced. Game here will be served alongside some of the freshest vegetables you'll ever come across.

Tommy Banks
Chef Patron

Did you know?

The Black Swan created it's own Italian style bitters, similar to Aperol and Campari by using an abundance of rhubarb from the chef's garden along with lemon verbena, tangerine marigold and foraged woodruff.

MICHELIN STAR

www.blackswanoldstead.co.uk

Oldstead
York
North Yorkshire YO61 4BL
T: 01347 868387
E: enquiries@blackswanoldstead.co.uk

THE BLACK SWAN AT OLDSTEAD

The Chester Grosvenor

Hotel, Restaurant & Spa

Cheshire

This famous old hotel in Chester has held a Michelin star since 1990. It is owned by The Duke of Westminster and by association has strong links to game and shooting - the family own a grouse shoot in Lancashire at Abbeystead. Chef Simon Radley first worked at the hotel back in 1986 and after spells abroad and in London took over in 1998.

With an outstanding cellar of fine wine and a really dedicated chef any visitor can be assured of high-class game cookery with the grouse season being a highlight.

Simon Radley
Executive Chef

Did you know?

The Chester Grosvenor looks out at Eastgate and its famous clock: The Eastgate Clock. It is said The Eastgate Clock is the most photographed clock in Britain after Big Ben.

MICHELIN STAR

www.chestergrosvenor.com

Grosvenor Shopping Centre
Eastgate Street
Chester CH1 1LT
T: 01244 324024
E: Hotel@ChesterGrosvenor.com

Simon Radley
THE CHESTER GROSVENOR

The Cinnamon Club

Restaurant

London

Set in the historic Grade II listed former Westminster Library, The Cinnamon Club is an institution in the world of Indian fine dining with a long history of serving innovative and creative Indian cuisine. Chef Vivek Singh and Head Chef Sankar Chandrasekaran have set new levels of creativity with game playing a central part on the new menus.

Game classics are often carved and served table-side with the tandoor playing an important part - tandoori venison saddle with pickling sauce demonstrates how classical Indian cookery suits game so well.

"Rajastani rulers were tribes of warriors who often indulged in hunting and so have a tradition of cooking with game including deer, wild boar, partridges and sand grouse."

Vivek Singh
Executive Chef

www.cinnamonclub.com

The Old Westminster Library
30-32 Great Smith Street
London SW1P 3BU
T: 020 7222 2555
E: info@cinnamonclub.com

THE CINNAMON CLUB

Interview

The Lincolnshire Game Company

Tristan and Simon

"Lincolnshire Game are market leaders in taking shot game and processing it. We talked to director, Simon Wilkinson, to discover why this is so important to get right. It turns out the future of shooting and game depends on it.

"Game is a very simple proposition but take away one market and the whole shooting industry crashes. If the UK supermarkets stopped taking game, there would be no more shooting – shoots would have to bury it.

"2-3 birds out of 10 after being shot and processed are good enough to stay as a whole bird for the supermarkets due to the visual quality. The remaining 7 don't. Part of the reason for this is bruising and damaging, as well as falling from height or a hard-mouthed dog.

"It's important to remember that businesses like ours are not game dealers We are food processors, and we pride ourselves on keeping the supply chain going. One of the things we rely on is volume. We need that because the percentages of whole game are so small. That means that our business is main what we would call carcass utilisation - using up what is left when the breasts have been taken off.

"There's a big market for cuts of meat as opposed to whole birds. We do over 50 tonnes per year of paté meat – cuts like thighs - which we then sell into the EU market. Our processing team is highly trained to be rigorous and expert at the grading process. Game is so varied that we need trained eyes to look at absolutely everything.

"We have over 50 employees including graders and technical managers and for that reason we can supply retailers like Fortnum & Mason and Harrods and restaurants like The Jugged Hare, Ottolenghi, and Le Gavroche. They need to be certain they are getting the best, consistently."

The Cross at Kenilworth

Restaurant

Warwickshire

The Cross at Kenilworth is the sister restaurant of Simpsons in Birmingham and is home to chef Adam Bennett who is one of the few chefs to actually represent his country at international level. Bennett is an accomplished chef with a strong pedigree in fine dining - he was head chef at Simpsons for 10 years before moving to The Cross and now holds a Michelin Star.

The Cross is a classic gastropub where you can expect high standards but in a relaxed setting with food and wine to match.

"I love game meat because it's totally natural, on our doorstep and gives us a great palate of flavours with which to work. Game is a highlight of the transition of summer through to autumn and my favourite season of the year."

Adam Bennett

Head Chef

MICHELIN STAR

www.thecrosskenilworth.co.uk

16 New Street
Kenilworth
CV8 2EZ
T: 01926 853840
E: enquiries@thecrosskenilworth.co.uk

THE CROSS
Kenilworth

The Dining Room at Whatley Manor

Hotel, Restaurant & Spa

Gloucestershire

Whatley Manor is located in the Cotswolds and is set in 12 acres of gardens with a long tree-lined driveway. There's a spa as well as rooms and two Michelin stars in The Dining Room headed up by Great British Menu star Niall Keating.

What sort of food can you expect? Keating's background says a lot: Restaurant Sat Bains, Benu in San Francisco and Restaurant Kong Hans Kaelder in Copenhagen. That's about as modern and refined as it gets. Combined with his love of game you'll be in for a treat.

Niall Keating
Executive Chef

There are six gardens at Whatley to enjoy. There's a kitchen garden and a stable courtyard, You can also find a herbaceous and rose garden as well as a loggia garden and a hot garden.

2 MICHELIN STAR · SUSTAINABLE GASTRONOMY

www.whatleymanor.com

Easton Grey
Malmesbury
Wiltshire SN16 0RB
T: 01666 822 888
E: reservations@whatleymanor.com

the dining room
whatley manor

The Chef's Table at The Dorchester

Hotel & Restaurant

London

For one of the most intimate game experiences anywhere in the UK we just had to list the chef's table at The Dorchester Hotel.

The specially designed room off the main kitchen gives you all the excitement of a busy kitchen yet is intimate enough for an unforgettable dinner.

Hotel Executive Chef Mario Perera is a game lover with a special affinity for venison and all its trimmings and he likes nothing more to have game on the menu at The Chef's Table. Look out for his venison ravioli.

"I love venison, it is my favourite game meat and regularly features on both my banqueting and chefs table menus at The Dorchester. My signature dish has to be venison ravioli with fig and pistachio crumble and Marsala jus - The flavour is delicious and these ingredients compliment each other so very well."

Mario Perera

Executive Chef

www.dorchestercollection.com

53 Park Lane
Mayfair
London W1K 1QA
T: 020 7629 8888
E: info.TDL@dorchestercollection.com

The Dorchester

Dorchester Collection

The Duck at Pett Bottom

Pub & Restaurant

Kent

Owned by South African born chef Dean Legg The Duck Inn near Canterbury is a classic English pub set in the Kent countryside. Dean spent his youth learning to cook on open fires back home before continuing his passion for cooking in local restaurants, The 26 and The Beacon in Tunbridge Wells.

Food at The Duck is plentiful and seasonal with game a feature during the autumn and winter. Guests can also expect to find Nordic influences on the menu with Magnus Nilsson of Faviken a hero in the kitchen.

"We're incredibly lucky to be surrounded by some of England's best countryside and with that comes our local shoot groups. Not only as regulars of the pub but they supply us with the freshest most amazing game, from fallow deer to pheasant and the humble pigeon. We're huge on local suppliers at the pub and when they're literally bringing it in from a shoot, you can't ask for better."

Dean Legg - Chef Patron

www.theduckpettbottom.com

Pett Bottom Road
Canterbury
CT4 5PB
T: 01227 830354
E: theduckpettbottom@outlook.com

The Dysart Petersham

Restaurant

London

The Dysart cleverly manages to be a country pub in the town. It sits on the edge of Richmond Park and has a bright and generous dining area with tables nicely spread apart.

What sets The Dysart apart is Kenneth Culhane, the chef in the kitchen. His brand of Asian-influenced fine dining mixed with a classical background is what attracted Michelin who gave it a star in 2019. Wild and local ingredients feature on the menu with game very much a part of the ethos. There's also a beautiful piano which is used for classical concerts.

"My childhood, on a remote farm in Southern Ireland, was pivotal towards instilling in me an understanding of good husbandry and of the top quality produce that only comes from a true understanding of the particular qualities of the land, the soil and nature, now a natural harmony for me. Game is an integral part of our rural heritage, I certainly remember this growing up. It truly sets us apart the from other cultural traditions, the quality in Ireland and the UK is unparalleled. In ecological terms, and with proper and strict controls, it is a force for good in the conservation of bird populations and restoration of natural countryside."

Kenneth Culhane
Head Chef

MICHELIN STAR

www.thedysartpetersham.co.uk

135 Petersham Road
London
TW10 7AA
T: 0208 9408005
E: enquiries@thedysartpetersham.co.uk

THE DYSART
PETERSHAM

The East End Arms

Restaurant with Rooms

Hampshire

The East End Arms is a charming New Forest Inn with a fascinating history.

It was bought by the Dire Straits bass player, John Illsley in 1990 to preserve it for the local community and is still going strong. In the kitchen game lover Ian Gibbs keeps up the local tradition of souring everything for the menu from as close to the Inn as possible.

We spotted a pressed game terrine on a recent menu. Guests can also stay over and there's an interesting wine list by Helen McGinn of the "Knackered Mothers Wine Club."

"It's so natural for us to use our local game and produce which is located around the New Forest, Hampshire and Dorset. There's deer, pigeon and pheasant. These are regulars on the menu. It's just lovely to know our ingredients are within a short distance, fresh and honest, whilst keeping our food miles as low as we can"

Ian Gibbs
Head Chef

www.eastendarms.co.uk

East End
Lymington
SO41 5SY
T: 01590 626223
E: info@eastendarms.co.uk

EAST END ARMS

The Elder

Restaurant

Bath & North East Somerset

Basically The Elder is game central. Situated within Hotel Indigo in Bath the restaurant handles not only game but also its butchery.

The Elder was founded on the principle of enjoyment of authentic, honest and timeless British cooking with Executive Chef Gavin Edney at the helm in the kitchen.

Game supremo Mike Robinson is The Elder's owner and provider of the game on the menu. A private garden supplies the seasonal fruit and vegetables.

All in all if you are after a rendition of what British game is all about - look no further.

"The British countryside is my larder and I feel very lucky for that. We produce such sensational wild meat in this country and with Mike Robinson, a pioneer in the field, being the owner of The Elder we have the highest quality produce available here. Beautiful produce being served in a beautiful setting."

Gavin Edney

Executive Chef

www.theelder.co.uk

2-8 South Parade
Bath
BA2 4AB
T: 01225 530 616
E: enquiries@theelder.co.uk

The ELDER BATH

Venison Wellington

by Charlotte Vincent

Head Chef at The Five Bells

Ingredients Serves 4

FOR THE PHEASANT

- 500g of loin of venison, cleaned with sinew removed
- 400g of puff pastry
- 2 egg yolk
- 1 tbsp of milk
- Salt
- Pepper
- 1 tbsp of vegetable oil

MUSHROOM DUXELLE

- 250g of button mushrooms
- 4 shallots, chopped
- 2 garlic cloves, chopped
- 100ml of white wine
- 4 tbsp of double cream
- Butter
- Salt
- Pepper

PANCAKES

- 150g of plain flour
- 2 eggs
- 140ml of milk
- Oil

Wine Pairing See page 165

Method

1. Start by searing the venison. Heat the oil in a large frying pan, season the loin with salt and pepper and add to the pan. Turn every 1-2 minutes to colour the loin on all sides, until it is evenly browned and rare in the centre. Remove from the pan and refrigerate.
2. For the duxelle, melt the butter in the same pan, add the chopped mushrooms and sauté until golden brown. Remove from the pan and keep to one side.
3. Add the shallots and chopped garlic to the pan. Cook until soft then add the mushrooms again and cook quickly until the liquid evaporates. Add the white wine and boil until reduced by half.
4. Add the cream and cook until the mixture is thick and beginning to darken. Season with salt and pepper and leave to one side.
5. For the pancakes, whisk together the flour, eggs and milk to make a smooth batter.
6. Heat a frying pan and add a splash of oil. Once the oil is hot, pour in a small amount of batter to cover the base in a very thin layer and cook until golden on the underside.
7. Flip the pancake over and cook the other side. Repeat the process again until all of the mixture is used up, keeping the cooked pancakes to one side.
8. Lay a sheet of cling film on a board and lay 3 pancakes onto it, overlapping so that they cover the cling film. Lay the Parma ham on top in a single layer.
9. Spread the mushroom duxelle over the Parma ham in another even layer and place the venison on top. Roll the pancakes, Parma ham and mushroom mix around the venison, using the cling film to wrap it tightly. Leave to cool in the fridge, preferably overnight.
10. Roll out the puff pastry into a thin sheet around 1/4 cm thick - if it is pre-rolled it will need to be rolled thinner.
11. Remove the Wellington from the cling film, lay on top of the pastry and brush the borders of the pastry with egg wash. Roll the Wellington in the pastry, sealing the joining edge with a little extra egg wash.
12. Roll the Wellington so the seal is on the underside and set aside while you prepare the vegetables.
13. Preheat the oven to 180°C/gas mark 4.
14. Place the Wellington into the oven for 20-25 minutes, until the pastry is golden brown. To tell if it is cooked, place a thin metal skewer in the centre of the venison, it should be slightly warm (which means the internal temperature is about 49-52°C).
15. Remove the Wellington from the oven, rest for at least 10 minutes in a warm place. Slice and serve up onto a plate.
16. I serve with redcurrant and game jus and rich green leafy vegetables tossed in butter and rock salt (triple cooked chips optional).

The Five Bells

Pub & Restaurant

Devon

Located in the sleepy village of Clyst Hydon, The Five Bells Inn is a beautiful thatched farmhouse offering award-winning fine dining mixed with traditional pub classics.

Home of Devon's 'Best Sunday Roast', the pub is located 11 miles from Exeter and has a cosy atmosphere with real ales, Devon ciders and locally produced food. In the kitchen ex pastry chef at Gidleigh Park Charlotte Vincent took over in 2019 and brings twenty years of experience to the role. Charlotte's style in her own words is classic contemporary with both specials and pub classics adorning the menu.

"At our heart we're a country pub and it's always a pleasure to chalk up game specials as and when they are available to us whether that be pheasant, rabbit, partridge or majestic cuts of wild venison. Provenance is everything and our food tells the story of the surrounding countryside."

Charlotte Vincent
Head Chef

DOG FRIENDLY

www.fivebells.uk.com

Clyst Hydon
Nr Cullompton
EX15 2NT
T: 01884 277288
E: info@fivebells.uk.com

the FIVE BELLS Inn

Willo Game

Nick Jones - Specialist Game Dealer Processor of Wild Game

"The guns have gone home after a good days shoot but that isn't the end of the journey for the game birds. They now go through a rigorous process on their way to market and into kitchens. This is where businesses like Willo Game come into their own. We spoke to Nick James, a director of Willo Game to find out more.

"Each shoot collection has a batch number, and this makes every bird traceable. This is very important. If there is a problem down the line then an EHO can work back and identify the source.

"Temperature-controlled vans pick up the birds from the shoots and always ensure that the birds are handled properly. The temperature of the vans is checked on leaving and arrival back at HQ.

"Bad handling is dangerous. We are dealing with food and it must be handled correctly. We applaud the BGA accreditation and are fully behind it and only buy from BGA assured shoots. It is important we get a good product.

So, when birds are first shot, they are hot in temperature. On a wet day, if the birds are piled on top of each other, the meat can get tarnished due to fungal infection in the feathers. They must be chilled properly.

We use a hot wax dip to remove all trace of feathers after they are plucked and eviscerated mechanically. They are then air-cooled, and the wax broken off to get rid of any remnants of the feathers.

Chefs often demand fresh not frozen, however with investment in a state-of-the-art blast freezer, we say 'frozen is the new fresh!' There is never any danger of running out of product and it is much easier for chefs to offer game on their menus with modern freezing technology."

www.willogame.co.uk

The Fox Inn Corscombe

Pub & Restaurant

Dorset

Mark Hix needs no introduction to food lovers in the UK. For many years his London restaurants celebrated simply-cooked and outstandingly thought-out dishes that were copied endlessly in other restaurants.

Today Mark Hix can be found in his home county of Dorset at The Fox Inn where guests can stay and enjoy simple home-cooked food done in the traditional style. Game features on the menu and is always done as it should be and accompanied by whatever is available that expresses it best.

Mark Hix

Chef Patron

In case you didn't know

Mark's Kitchen Library can be book for up to 10 people. Here you'll be surrounded by Mark Hix's collection of over 2,000 cookbooks, antiques and curiosities and eat in front of the Aga.

www.thefoxinncorscombe.co.uk

Pound Hill
Corscombe
Dorset DT2 0NS
T: 01935 317555
E: reservations@thefoxinncorscombe.co.uk

THE FOX INN

The Freemasons at Wiswell

Restaurant with Rooms

Lancashire

The Freemasons takes dining in a pub to a new level. Located in the Ribble Valley village of Wiswell, not far from iconic Pendle Hill in Lancashire chef Steve Smith's powerhouse of dining out takes centre stage. The various dining areas are traditional but you can opt for the ultra modern Mr Smith's kitchen table and get a glimpse of the action. The food is classic with modern twists and Steve Smith's irrepressible touches are everywhere. Game features during the season and seasonal menus are varied in styles with the tasting menu a popular option.

"Local produce and seasonality is of real importance to us – our game is all locally sourced and brings a real richness and diversity to our menus. Our Glorious 12th event gives us the opportunity to create some truly special dishes, which both showcase and celebrate the local area.

Steven Smith

Chef Patron

DOG FRIENDLY

www.freemasonsatwiswell.com

8 Vicarage Fold
Wiswell
Clitheroe
Lancashire BB7 9DF
T: 01254 822 218 E: enquiries@freemasonswiswell.co.uk

FREEMASONS AT WISWELL

The Game Bird at The Stafford

Hotel & Restaurant

London

A charming contemporary British restaurant, located within The Stafford Hotel in London's St James's, that focusses on game in season as well as new renditions of classic dishes. Overseen by chef Ben Tish and Stafford Hotel executive chef Josef Rogulski, The Game Bird is everything a game lover could want in a restaurant.

An exclusive setting, the best game of all varieties, amazing wine and service with a light touch. Beside the game you'll find steak and ale pudding, smoked fish pie and smoked eel carved at your table.

"I love the versatility of game. There are so many different flavours. My favourite has to be wild mallard.

I confit the legs and serve the crown simply roasted to showcase the natural flavour. It's outstanding."

Jozef Rogulski
Executive Chef

www.thestaffordlondon.com

16-18 St James's Place
London
SW1A 1NJ
T: 0207 493 0111
E: reservations@thestaffordlondon.com

THE GAME BIRD
AT THE STAFFORD LONDON

The Gilpin

Hotel, Restaurant & Spa

Cumbria

Known simply as The Gilpin this Lake District favourite has managed to create the ultimate spa meets luxury hotel and dining retreat with an exceptional chef in the kitchen. Hrishikesh Desai is a talented Indian-born chef with a unique ability to bring freshness and spice into everything he cooks.

Trained classically with stints including at The French Laundry in California (a former World's 50 Best Restaurant winner) Hrishi, as he is fondly known, won a Michelin star recently. When game is on the menu either at the main restaurant or in Gilpin Spice you can be assured it will be perfectly treated.

"British game is an integral part of British gastronomy which has evolved through time. There are excellent game keepers in Britain who with full dedication ensure that the game is sustainable and looked after. It is very important that chefs showcase this game and the gamekeepers on their menu to promote what is best in Britain."

Hrishikesh Desai
Executive Chef

MICHELIN STAR

www.thegilpin.co.uk

Crook Road
Windermere
LA23 3NE
T: 01539 488818
E: hotel@thegilpin.co.uk

gilpin

The Glenturret Lalique Restaurant

Restaurant

Perthshire

The Glenturret Lalique Restaurant is new but sufficiently exciting for it to include a mention straightaway. Located at the Glenturret Distillery in Perthshire, Scotland's oldest working distillery, the Lalique restaurant will be dinner only. However, you can expect game to be one of the star ingredients.

The kitchens will be headed up by chef Mark Donald who was, most recently, the head chef at Number One at The Balmoral in Edinburgh but he is no stranger to high-level cooking with spells at Restaurant Andrew Fairlie, Noma in Copenhagen and with Claude Bosi at Hibiscus.

"Having travelled the globe with exposure to the best produce available, I can confidently say that Scottish game is of world class quality. Now, more than ever before, not including game on our menu would be a huge misstep, not only failing to support local game suppliers but also detracting from our guest's experience. Being able to cook game in Perthshire which is often referred to as the "Jewel in the crown" of Scotland's fantastic larder is incredibly exciting and a luxury myself and the team do not take for granted."

Mark Donald
Executive Chef

www.theglenturret.com

The Glenturret Distillery
The Hosh, Crieff
Perthshire PH7 4HA
T: 01764 656565
E: enquiries@theglenturret.com

THE GLENTURRET
· LALIQUE RESTAURANT ·

The Goring

Hotel & Restaurant

London

Designed by David Linley, The Dining Room is bathed in natural light by day and sumptuously aglow with Swarovski chandeliers at night. It's a proper stage for Executive Chef Richard Galli to present his modern take on traditional British food.

The Goring is a privately owned 5 star hotel in Victoria close to Buckingham Palace and is an understated masterpiece. For those who know it, it is a secret they want to keep to themselves just because it's all so beautifully and simply done. In the game season you will find the classics done elegantly with refinement.

"We do extremely well for game in Britain. The different species give us a real tie to the seasons, starting with grouse in August, all the way through. I just love the varying flavours and textures and am a huge fan of venison.

My favourite feathered game has to be snipe, but sadly I see this less and less. You just can't beat the flavour of teal, woodcock and partridge, all unique in their own way - Wonderful natural treats that enable us to produce beautiful game dishes at The Goring."

Richard Galli
Executive Chef

MICHELIN STAR

www.thegoring.com

15 Beeston Place
London
SW1W 0JW
T: 020 7396 9000
E: reception@thegoring.com

The Goring

The Grove at Narberth

Hotel & Restaurant

Pembrokeshire

An enchanting country house that's quite unique - Jacobian, Victorian Arts and Crafts with thoughtful contemporary touches. Award-winning cuisine - it's a favourite with foodies too.

The Grove of Narberth is a privately owned luxury hotel nestled in the heart of the rolling Pembrokeshire countryside with stunning views of the Preseli Hills.

It was also The Sunday Times Hotel of the Year 2020. With beautiful gardens as well game-loving guests are in for a treat. In The Fernery Executive Head Chef Douglas Balish draws his inspiration from the location and is particularly fond of game in season.

Every detail of the restaurant interiors has been designed to reflect the ethos of the restaurant. The humble 'fern' characterises the local hedgerows and woodland.

"Game season is one of the most exciting times of the year. With the arrival of autumn it brings a warmth to the dishes we serve. The depth of flavour from game makes it a real treat to use in the kitchen and using it in our tasting menu gives the guests the opportunity to try something that they wouldn't have access to in most supermarkets."

Douglas Balish
Head Chef

DOG FRIENDLY

www.thegrove-narberth.co.uk

Narberth
Pembrokeshire
Wales
SA67 8BX

GROVE
NARBERTH

T: 01834 860 915 E: reservations@grovenarberth.co.uk

The Gunton Arms

Pub & Restaurant

Norfolk

You're off to a good start when the description on the website says this: "Opened October 2011, The Gunton Arms is a traditional pub with 12 bedrooms in an extensive historic park near Cromer in North Norfolk.

The chef Stuart Tattersall (ex head chef at Mark Hix) cooks from local ingredients including venison from the surrounding deer park." Leather sofas, log fires, good food, game on the menu, excellent chef, good beers and wines. All in a majestic setting. That's all you need to know to want to visit this brilliant pub.

Stuart Tattershall
Head Chef

The Gunton Arms is situated in the one thousand acre deer park which surrounds Gunton Hall near Cromer in Norfolk. The park was created in the early 18th Century by the Harbord family and was comparable in scale to the great estates to the west, Holkham and Houghton.

www.theguntonarms.co.uk

Cromer Road
Thorpe Market
Norwich NR11 8TZ
T: 01263 832010
E: office@theguntonarms.co.uk

THE GUNTON ARMS

The Hand & Flowers

Pub & Restaurant with Rooms

Buckinghamshire

The signature pub of TV chef Tom Kerridge who is now the last word on pub grub. But underneath the chummy exterior is a fine chef and the food at The Hand and Flowers, located in Marlow, is refined and carefully thought out despite its traditional appearance.

Restaurants like this don't get to 2 Michelin stars very easily so visitors can be assured of the standards before they walk in. When it's on the menu, game will be every bit as appealing and well done as the famous fish and chips.

Tom Kerridge
Chef Patron

Did you know?

Tom Kerridge is married to Beth Cullen-Kerridge who is a sculptor who attended the Royal College of Art. In 1994, she became the first artist to be presented with the commission for the Napoleon Garden Sculpture exhibition in Holland Park. Her work was subsequently shown in two of the London Parks.

2 MICHELIN STAR

www.thehandandflowers.co.uk

126 West Street
Marlow
SL7 2BP
T: 01628 482277
E: contact@thehandandflowers.co.uk

The Hand & Flowers

The Hardwick

Restaurant with Rooms

Monmouthshire

Stephen Terry's The Hardwick is one of those restaurants that is worth travelling out of your way for. Located near Abergavenny it has been delighting guests for many years.

Terry himself is an accomplished chef who started his career with Marco Pierre White and you can still see those influences on his menu. This is food done classically but in a signature style and the menu is full of ideas and expression.

When it comes to game you can expect the full treatment from duck hash to terrines and braised rabbit with everything in season getting a look in.

"The whole thing about game for me is its seasonality and I whole-heartedly look forward to the game season. I love everything about it; from the different species as the season progresses to the abundance of delicious veg that grows at the same time, it all grows and goes together perfectly. I very much enjoy the ritual of going out on a shoot too and have previously been out with fellow game loving chefs James Martin, Paul Ainsworth and Galton Blackiston who are all in this guide!"

Stephen Terry
Chef Patron

www.thehardwick.co.uk

Old Raglan Road
Abergavenny
NP7 9AA
T: 01873 854220
E: info@thehardwick.co.uk

the HARDWICK

The Jugged Hare

Pub & Restaurant

London

There are more than a handful of venues in this guide that are really excellent for game but I'll leave it to The Jugged Hare, situated next to The Barbican, to describe itself because it says all you need to know, succinctly: London's leading game restaurant prides itself on full flavours, innovative ideas and perfectly executed dishes at every service.

From classic cuts and succulent steaks to squirrel croquettes and crispy crumbed pheasant, a focus on both traditional and lesser-known (but always seasonal), British ingredients served alongside independent boutique wines makes this handsome gastro pub a game-changing drinking and dining spot for the City.

Steve Englefield

Head Chef

The Jugged Hare is located right next to The Barbican Centre which was created from the bombed remnants of Cripplegate after the Second World War. Cripplegate had been a centre for the rag trade.

www.thejuggedhare.com

49 Chiswell Street
London
EC1Y 4SA
T: 020 8161 0190
E: info@thejuggedhare.com

THE JUGGED HARE

The Kingham Plough

Pub & Restaurant

Oxfordshire

The Kingham Plough, in Chipping Norton, was made famous by former Great British Menu winner Emily Watkins who championed local ingredients from the Cotswolds and built up a formidable following.

The pub now continues where she left off with Head Chef, Johnny Pons, formerly of Slaughters Country Inn, Ellenborough Park Hotel and The Feathered Nest in charge of a daily-changing modern menu of British dishes with Mediterranean influences and British pub classics. There's good beer from Hook Norton, two lovely dining rooms and game on the classic menu to enjoy.

"Living and cooking in the Cotswolds brings you naturally closer to nature. Using what's at are finger tips and is in season is what has always been at the essence of the plough. Game is undoubtedly a unique and hardy ingredient. Sustainable and delicious."

Johnny Pons
Head Chef

www.thekinghamplough.co.uk

The Green, Kingham
Chipping Norton
Oxfordshire OX7 6YD
T: 01608 658327
E: book@thekinghamplough.co.uk

THE KINGHAM PLOUGH

The Kings Arms Inn

Pub & Restaurant

Leicestershire

A previous winner at the Eat Game Awards (2019) The Kings Arms in Wing, Rutland, serves traditional, artisan and innovative pub fare on rustic wooden kitchen tables, surrounded by beamed ceilings, flagstone floors & open fires.

The bar brims with a large selection of homemade snacks from Jimmy's Rutland Smokehouse.

Bottles of homemade sloe gin, elderflower vodka and Zermatter mulled wine are all made with berries from the surrounding hedgerows and fruit from neighbours.

"Our pub restaurant is born of the surrounding countryside, those working it, and its flora & fauna. Field to fork and nose to tail are the mantras we live by. These relationships are all interlinked and tied together by Game, we love to be part of that community."

James Goss
Chef Patron

www.thekingsarms-wing.co.uk

13 Top Street
Wing
Rutland LE15 8SE
T: 01572 737634
E: info@thekingsarms-wing.co.uk

KING'S ARMS
WING
INN & RESTAURANT

The Kitchin

Restaurant

Edinburgh

Tom and Michaela Kitchin opened their restaurant, The Kitchin on Edinburgh's Leith waterfront in 2006. They won a Michelin star in 2007. The Kitchin is all about British seasonal cuisine influenced by French cooking techniques (Tom Kitchin trained under renowned Pierre Koffmann).

The whole philosophy of the food is the idea of 'From Nature to Plate', and this a true reflection of Tom's passion for the finest, freshest Scottish seasonal produce. Game features strongly on the menu with hare, grouse, wild duck and others all making a recent menu example.

Tom Kitchin

Chef Patron

Michaela Kitchin has a BSc Hons degree in Hotel & Restaurant Management from University of Surrey and more than 15 years of hospitality experience having worked in her native Sweden, with Anton Mosimann in London, Savoy London, The Savoy Group and at the world-famous 7-star hotel Burj Al Arab in Dubai before the couple settled in Tom's home town of Edinburgh.

MICHELIN STAR

www.thekitchin.com

78 Commercial Quay
Leith
Edinburgh EH6 6LX
T: 0131 555 1755
E: info@thekitchin.com

THE KITCHIN

The Lamb at Longdown

Pub & Restaurant

Devon

A few minutes outside Exeter, in the heart of rolling Devon countryside you'll find The Lamb at Longdown run by local chef Dolton Lodge.

The philosophy here is simple: get all the ingredients from as close to the pub as possible and if not make sure they're up to scratch. We've tried to get a nice balance of pubs and restaurants in The Great Game Guide.

Some are just simple examples of where game is served in a nice way and that's what you'll find at The Lamb at Longdown.

"Game of all types is all around us here at The Lamb. We are a stones throw from Perridge Estate and an abundance of local shoots. We are lucky to be able to cook with such amazing produce and to let our creativity flow."

Dolton Lodge

Chef Patron

www.thelamblongdown.co.uk

Longdown
Exeter
EX6 7SR
T: 01392 811 100
E: thelamblongdown@gmail.com

The Lamb
LONGDOWN

The Manor House

Hotel & Restaurant

Wiltshire

Taking its name from the river that runs through the hotel grounds, the Michelin starred Bybrook restaurant enjoys a beautiful setting.

The kitchen, headed up by Executive Chef Robert Potter, creates seasonal dishes from local ingredients, enhanced by wines of the world.

Potter worked for Dominic Chapman at The Royal Oak Paley Street and then under Hywel Jones at Lucknam Park. He is, therefore, very well versed in country house cooking and you'll find it in spades at The Manor House.

"It's great to be noted specifically for our use of game! There is always an expectation to offer the best produce our local larder provides and with The Manor House being set in beautiful countryside we're particularly excited when game season comes around."

Robert Potter
Executive Chef

MICHELIN STAR

www.exclusive.co.uk

Castle Combe
Chippenham
Wiltshire SN14 7HX
T: 01249 782206
E: themanorhouse@exclusive.co.uk

THE MANOR HOUSE

The Masons Arms

Pub & Restaurant

Devon

If you happened on The Masons Arms without knowing about it you'd probably describe it as the quintessential thatched pub. It certainly looks gorgeous. But chocolate boxes need exciting centres and inside is where it matters here.

Chef Mark Dodson was head chef at The Waterside Inn under the late Michel Roux OBE and that means the food on offer is first class. The Michelin star attests to that. You'll find game on the menu through the season and you can expect it to be give due respect and handled with real skill.

"I love cooking game as it really fits in with our ethos. It is completely seasonal and local. We use a wide selection of game during the season, both feathered and furred. Game is so versatile, from beautiful terrines, patês and pies, thick soups and stews to the most delicate of consommés. We should all eat and enjoy more game!"

Mark Dodson
Chef Patron

MICHELIN STAR

www.masonsarmsdevon.co.uk

Knowstone
South Molton
Devon EX36 4RY
T: 01398 341231
E: enqs@masonsarmsdevon.co.uk

THE MASONS ARMS
KNOWSTONE

The Olive Tree

Restaurant

Bath & North East Somerset

Known for being one of Bath's longest established independent restaurants, The Olive Tree Restaurant – located below the luxurious Queensberry Hotel on Russel Street – was awarded its first Michelin star in October 2018.

This distinction is in addition to the restaurant's 3 AA Rosette status. In the kitchen chef Chris Cleghorn has his own style that takes advantage of being part of the South West's excellent supplier database. The food at The Olive Tree is eclectic and stylish which is fitting for its location. Game features but is given the modern treatment.

"I couldn't imagine not having game on one of my menus when the season calls for it. It adds so much in terms of flavour profile and it's so versatile. It can be complemented by other seasonal fruits and vegetables available as part of an all-round hearty seasonal dish."

Chris Cleghorn
Executive Chef

MICHELIN STAR

www.olivetreebath.co.uk

The Queensberry Hotel
Russel Street
Bath BA1 2QF
T: 01225 447928
E: reservations@thequeensberry.co.uk

OLIVE Tree RESTAURANT

The Peat Inn

Restaurant with Rooms

Fife

Sometimes the stars align and a combination of location, building, chef and ingredients all come together to form a perfect whole.

To visit The Peat Inn is to visit Scotland and Scotland has great ingredients and great game. Chef proprietor Geoffrey Smeddle has held a Michelin star at The Peat Inn since 2010 and is widely regarded to be one of the best chefs in Scotland. This style of restaurant with rooms has really led the way in hospitality in recent years and anyone venturing into golfing country round St Andrews only wants to eat at one place and that's The Peat Inn.

"Scotland is justly famous for its wonderful larder of word class ingredients which we are proud to showcase. But the crowning glory of them all is wild game. Fragrant grouse, tender roe deer and succulent partridge are always featured in season, a joy to cook and an indulgence to eat."

Geoffrey Smeddle
Chef Patron

MICHELIN STAR

www.thepeatinn.co.uk

Peat Inn
Near St Andrew's
Fife KY15 5LH
T: 01334 840206
E: stay@thepeatinn.co.uk

the Peat Inn
RESTAURANT WITH ROOMS

The Raby Hunt

Restaurant with Rooms

County Durham

Two Michelin stars, a chef on a mission, out in the sticks in the North East. There's plenty going on at this cutting edge restaurant that's taking fine dining in new directions. Chef James Close's food will take you in every direction except the obvious.

There's a fifteen course tasting menu and a kitchen table and the chocolates at the end are called skulls which are a collaboration between James Close and pastry chef Maria Guseva. Whichever way you look at it The Ruby Hunt is a completely unmatched experience. And that goes for game, too.

James Close
Chef Patron

James Close taught himself to cook in his late twenties after he gave up on his dream to be a golf pro. He learnt from books and also visiting restaurants and eating his way through the menu. From there it was simple trial and error.

2 MICHELIN STAR

www.rabyhuntrestaurant.co.uk

Summerhouse
Darlington
County Durham DL2 3UD
T: 01325 374237
E: enquiries@rabyhuntrestaurant.co.uk

THE RABY HUNT RESTAURANT AND ROOMS

The Rigbye Arms

Pub & Restaurant

Lancashire

A game-loving pub if ever there was one! The Rigbye Arms sits on High Moor Lane outside Parbold in Lancashire and takes pride in its special game menu which is available through the year but more abundantly in season. You'll find pheasant wrapped in bacon, partridge Wellington, crispy pheasant goujons, duck, grouse and venison.

The Rigbye Arms is fortunate enough to be close to a number of game shoot estates and through chef patron David Jones the kitchen is able to source the highest quality game.

David Jones
Chef Patron

A walk before dinner?

If you get chance take in the Parbold Hill Circuit where you will see The Pennine Hills, Harrock Hill and Hunter's Hill. At the top on a clear day you can see Liverpool, Blackpool Tower and the Berwyn mountains of North Wales.

www.rigbyearms.com

2 Whittle Lane
Wrightington
Wigan WN6 9QB
T: 01257 462354
E: info@rigbyearms.com

The Rigbye Arms

The Ritz Restaurant

Hotel & Restaurant

London

To dine in The Ritz is to step back in time. The big windows that give way to a view of Green Park, the luxury-laden tables and the smartly-attired staff all contribute to a unique experience.

And in John Williams The Ritz has a chef who fully lives up to the role. The menu gives a glimpse into the "Belle Epoque" of French cuisine but with the flair and ingredients of an English chef in his prime.

Expect any game on the menu to be flawless - but go for the grouse. It's chef's favourite.

"Game is massively important to me in our kitchen. I love wild food because it has a natural flavour that comes from the natural environment which gives it a distinctive flavour and seasonality."

John Williams MBE

Executive Chef

Photo credit: © John Carey

MICHELIN STAR

www.theritzlondon.com

150 Piccadilly
London
W1J 9BR
T: 020 7493 8181
E: enquire@theritzlondon.com

THE RITZ LONDON

The Small Holding

Pub & Restaurant

Kent

There are only 26 covers at The Small Holding, but those who can get a booking are in for a treat. The menu is defined by what's available and served as a tasting experience. Set in one acre of its own land the former pub not only cooks locally but rears and grows its own. Owner Will Devlin is a game fan and all types of game feature through the season. The kitchen garden grows over 200 varieties of vegetables and fruits that are harvested specifically for the menu. Rare breed pigs, chickens and ducks roam around nearby.

"People can be put off game as tough and overly strong in flavour, but we need to forget that. Game birds such as pheasant, grouse, partridge, and mallard live off the land in the countryside, eating naturally, meaning they are more ethical and have superior flavour."

Will Devlin

Chef Patron

SUSTAINABLE GASTRONOMY

www.thesmallholding.restaurant

Ranters Lane
Kilndown
Kent TN17 2SG
T: 01892 890105
E: bookings@thesmallholding.restaurant

The SMALL HOLDING
Farm & Kitchen

The Sportsman

Pub & Restaurant

Kent

Stephen Harris took over The Sportsman in Seasalter, near Whitstable, Kent, on the Thames Estuary in 1999 with his brother Philip. The pub was awarded a Michelin star in 2008 which was the first of a string of subsequent awards. Stephen is one of those classic English cooks who just knows how to do things properly. In that sense he's very much in the same mould as Simon Hopkinson, Jenifer Paterson and even Elizabeth David.

The restaurant churns its own butter and the Thames Estuary provides oysters and fish, and in front, marshland, woods and fertile soils provide meat, vegetables and game.

Stephen Harris

Chef Patron

Did you know?

During the Second World War The Sportsman was the billet for a company of the 1st Battalion London Irish Rifles. In September 1940 these troops happened to successfully engage the crew of a crashed German airplane on nearby Graveney Marsh.

MICHELIN STAR

www.thesportsmanseasalter.co.uk

Faversham Road
Seasalter, Whitstable
Kent CT5 4BP
T: 01227 273370
E: sportsmanseasalter@googlemail.com

THE SPORTSMAN

The Stackpole Inn

Restaurant with Rooms

Pembrokeshire

Local provenance defines The Stackpole Inn near Pembroke in Wales and it can be seen on head chef Matt Waldron's menus. This is where he really gets to showcase the strong relationships with farmers and small local suppliers that have been built up over the years.

Over the past 12 years, Gary and Becky Evans and their team have won numerous awards and it's easy to see why. The Stackpole is a classic pub with rooms, simple in decor, elaborate in food and situated close to the Pembrokeshire coast.

"It's great to have a guide dedicated to game, featuring the top restaurants and chefs showcasing the best of British game. Seasonality and provenance are a massive part of what we do at The Stackpole Inn and our customers love the fact that we showcase the best that Wales has to offer."

Matt Waldron
Executive Chef

www.stackpoleinn.co.uk

Jason's Corner
Stackpole
Pembrokeshire SA71 5DF
T: 01646 672324
E: info@stackpoleinn.co.uk

THE STACKPOLE INN

The Star Inn

Restaurant with Rooms

Yorkshire

Andrew Pern's classic North Yorkshire village pub dates back to the 14th Century. Located in the quiet village of Harome, near Helmsley, Pern has been building The Star Inn into a gastro destination since 1996.

The pub has ben awarded just about everything and it's not hard to see why when you arrive: it's another of those gorgeous examples of British pubs that excel in doing things well. The Star Inn is essentially an Inn with Rooms serving 'modern Yorkshire' food made primarily from locally-sourced seasonal ingredients, such as local game, North Sea fish and fresh herbs from its own kitchen garden.

"The menus at The Star Inn are essentially written by the seasons and by the larder of God's Own Country. In Harome, we are surrounded by the produce used in our kitchens, including furred and feathered game from the nearby estates, so seasonal game will always feature on our menus."

Andrew Pern
Chef Patron

MICHELIN STAR

DOG FRIENDLY

www.thestaratharome.co.uk

High Street
Harome
York YO62 5JE
T: 01439 770397
E: reservations@thestarinnatharome.co.uk

The Star Inn

The West House

Restaurant with Rooms

Kent

The West House Restaurant with Rooms, housed in a 16th Century weaver's cottage in the village of Biddenden in the Weald of Kent, is the restaurant of chef patron Graham Garrett, a former rock and roll drummer.

Garrett may have come to cooking late but has never looked back. His food is celebrated far and wide for a couple of simple reasons: technical skill and an ability to find the best ingredients even when everyone is looking for the same thing. When game is on the menu you can be assured that its treatment will be precise.

"We should be eating more game because everyone talks about sustainability, but this is the most healthy meat there is. Venison is perhaps the healthiest red meat there is and we should be eating more game for so many reasons: Ethical, sustainable - Everyone wants to know where their meat is from and there is nothing more honest and tracable than game meat. We should be eating wild food, as opposed to intensively farmed meat full of antibiotics and chemicals."

Graham Garrett
Chef Patron

www.thewesthouserestaurant.co.uk

28 High Street
Biddenden
Ashford TN27 8AH
T: 01580 291341
E: thewesthouse@btconnect.com

The Woodsman

Pub & Restaurant

Warwickshire

Mike Robinson's homage to game and simple British cooking is in Stratford upon Avon a stone's throw from The Royal Shakespeare Company.

With a core field to fork philosophy The Woodsman menu is a celebration of a passion for wild food with game at the centre of the offering. Game is delivered from local estates and chefs source produce from local farmers, makers, foragers and from the pub's own botanical and herb garden. Much use is made of cooking with charcoal and flame using primarily oak and alder to lend a naturally sweet taste to the smoke.

"The Woodsman is all about bringing the outside in. British wild produce is sublime and we are lucky enough to have the perfect platform to serve it at its best.

We cook over coal and fire which perfectly suits the wild produce we love to cook."

Jon Coates
Head Chef

www.thewoodsmanrestaurant.com

No.4 Chapel Street
Stratford-Upon-Avon
Warwickshire CV37 6HA
T: 01789 331535
E: enquiries@thewoodsmanrestaurant.co.uk

THE WOODSMAN
Stratford-Upon-Avon

The Woodspeen

Restaurant

Berkshire

In 2013 a group of hospitality professionals got together to turn a run-down country pub into a beautiful, contemporary restaurant with a cosy bar. The reason was not obvious at first but as the renovation was finished the true scope of the idea could be seen: the breathtaking views over the West Berkshire countryside.

The Woodspeen has a cookery school and a chefs garden and a kitchen team that have won a Michelin star. You'll find plenty of game on the menu from carefully created ballotines to roasts all in a delightfully airy and bright room with open kitchen.

Peter Eaton
Executive Chef

25 Yards Gin

The Woodspeen has crafted its own gin called 25 Yards using botanicals from the kitchen garden which sits 25 yards from the restaurant. The result: a hand-crafted London dry gin.

MICHELIN STAR

www.thewoodspeen.com

Lambourn Road
Woodspeen
Newbury RG20 8BN
T: 01635 265070
E: hello@thewoodspeen.com

THE WOODSPEEN

Wood Restaurant

Restaurant

Greater Manchester

Simon Wood's restaurant in Manchester came about in 2017 after he won Masterchef in 2015. It's no easy thing to pull off a restaurant opening with little experience but Wood Restaurant has gone from strength to strength.

The idea was to create a unique style of non-intimidating high end dining. His style is bold as this mallard dish describes: Spiced Mallard | Tangerine Root | Vichy Grilled Carrot | Plum. Manchester chefs don't seem to feel the pressure of their London cousins and consequently the whole dining scene in the capital of the North is free and unencumbered.

"Game is so unique – the colour, the flavour and where it comes from. I love that it's wild and full of natural flavour.

It is so deliciously different. It deserves respect and you need to be careful how you treat it and buy it."

Simon Wood
Chef Patron

www.woodrestaurantgroup.com

Jack Rosenthal Street
First Street
Manchester M15 4RA
T: 0161 236 5211
E: info@woodmanchester.com

Interview

Nick Radclyffe

Foxdenton

When did your love affair with fruit gins begin?

I started shooting at the age of 11 and once old enough I was included in the elevenses ritual of Sloe gin. My fist sip of Sloe gin must have been in the mid-1970s and I remember thinking how wonderful to find something that tasted so lovely and warming. Fortunately, my father showed me how to make Sloe Gin very early in life so we have enjoyed that and it variants for decades now.

Why is it a tradition to take fruit liqueurs out on shoot days?

Reading some of my grandfathers writing on shoots one can see that serving fruit liqueurs has been a part of shooting since the Victorian era. The tradition started as a way to make time between the big drives of the morning as the beaters made their way from one drive to the next. It has been maintained as an excellent way to break up the morning drives and allow everyone to chat about the first drive and particularly get to know new guns or other guests. An important consideration is that while liqueurs are good at giving a perceived shot of warmth they are not high in alcohol and are usually served in small tots.

What is your favourite Foxdenton tipple to enjoy and why?

Hard question as we make many varieties and I really do like them all. However if I am out shooting I love Damson best of all as it combines tartness and sweetness perfectly. In the shoot lodge my favourite tipple

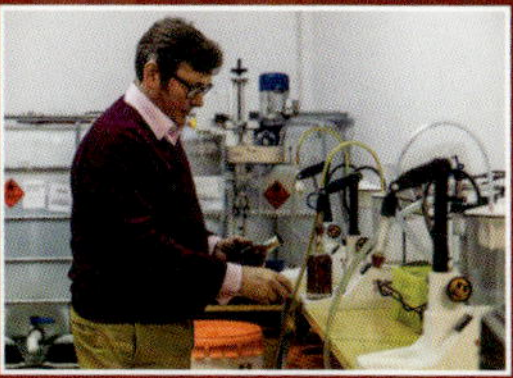

after a meal is our Golden Apricot made exclusively from English Apricots which is the perfect after dinner digestif for me.

Is there anything new on the agenda for Foxdenton in 2021/22?

We are always working on new ideas and flavours as we are constantly asked for interesting flavours. Coming soon will be a dryer lime gin liqueur which is great mixed as an aperitif and we have a new Hedgerow Gin liqueur due out late this year.

www.foxdentonestate.co.uk

Established 1935
Real Fruit. Real Flavour.
FOXDENTON
SPIRITS & LIQUEURS

Ynyshir

Restaurant with Rooms

Powys

Ynyshir might be the very last entry in this years Great Game Guide list but don't let that mean anything. Ynyshir near the Welsh town of Machynlleth in Powys is a powerhouse of a restaurant run by chef Gareth Ward (and his partner Amelia) in his own inimitable style. 5 AA rosettes and a Michelin star are just some of the awards the restaurant has achieved.

The website describes it as ingredient led, flavour driven, fat fuelled and meat obsessed. And that pretty much sums it up. Ynyshir is a trek but there are also rooms and in Gareth Ward's safe hands you are going to experience something special.

Gareth Ward

Chef Patron

Did you know?

In the 1840s the first deep coal mine was sunk in the Welsh village of Ynyshir. It was the first colliery to be opened in the Rhondda Fach valley. As a result Ynyshir represents the earliest colliery settlement of the valley

MICHELIN STAR

www.ynyshir.co.uk

Eglwys Fach
Powys
Wales SY20 8TA
T: 01654 781 209
E: info@ynyshir.co.uk

Ynyshir
Restaurant and Rooms

Photo credit: Daniel Burka - @dburka

The Retailers

Where to buy accredited game with confidence.

Quality game is not always available and due to Covid 19 and lockdown new ways of shopping will mean that more and more game will be available online going forward. Our short guide to where to buy game will help you decide where to look for it. Don't be surprised to see fishmongers on the list as this has traditionally been a common place to find all sorts of game birds in season.

Alan Pickup Quality Butchers
Cheshire
01928 733 232

Barony Country Foods
Lockerbie
01387811928
www.baronycountryfoods.co.uk

Bells Fishmongers
(CUMBRIAN Game)
Carlisle
01228 542924
www.bellsfishmongers.co.uk

C. Lidgate Butcher & Charcutier
London
020 7727 8243
www.lidgates.com

Casey Fields Farm Shop
Berkshire
01635 579662
www.caseyfieldsfarmshop.co.uk

Castle Game
Edinburgh
07967 133809
www.castlegame.co.uk

Cornwalls Family Butchers
Herefordshire
01989 562 216

Curtis Pitts Deer Services Ltd
Devon
07903 411657
www.curtispittsdeerservices.com

Deer Box
Newbury
03333 05 75 35
www.deerbox.co.uk

Farmison & Co
North Yorkshire
01765 824050
www.farmison.com

Field & Flower
Somerset
0203 735 8005
www.fieldandflower.co.uk

Furness Fish
Cumbria
015395 59544
www.morecambebayshrimps.com

Goodies Food Hall
Norflok
01379 676880

Harrods
London
020 7225 6800
www.harrods.com

HG Walter
London
020 7385 6466
www.hgwalter.com

Holme Farmed Venison
North Yorkshire
01977 686 440
www.hfv.co.uk

L & A Dent Game Dealers
Leyburn
07710 627181
www.dent-game-dealers.co.uk

Lodge Farm Kitchen
Herefordshire
01989 764422
www.lodgefarmkitchen.com

M C Kelly
Devon
01363 84545
www.mckelly.co.uk

Mayers Fishmongers
Blackburn
01254 669140
www.blackburnmarket.com

Mack & Wild
Scotland
www.macandwild.com

Wild Venison Haunch from **Farmison & Co**

Ox Close Fine Foods
Wetherby
07572 037428
www.oxclosefinefoods.co.uk

Pennant Valley Game
Powys
07896 141 779
www.wildwelshmeat.co.uk

Rhug Organic Farm
Denbighshire
01490 413 000
www.rhug.co.uk

RJ & RB Mailes Family Butcher
Herefordshire
01981 240234

Solent Butchers
Hampshire
02392 669228
www.solentbutchers.co.uk

South Downs Venison
West Sussex
01798 343245
www.southdownsvenison.co.uk

T. Harper & Son
Bedfordshire
01582 872001
www.harpersfood.co.uk

Taste Tradition
North Yorkshire
01765 608273
www.tastetradition.co.uk

Taywell Farm Shop
Kent
01580 211853
www.taywellfarm.co.uk

Thatchams Butchers
Berkshire
01635 33066
www.thatchambutchers.co.uk

The Exmoor Game Company
Taunton
07879 188 136
www.
theexmoorgamecompany.com

The Meat Box Company
Devon
01363 85905
www.themeatboxcompany.
co.uk

The Wild Meat Company
Saxmundham
01728 663458
www.wildmeat.co.uk

Truly Traceable
Suffolk
01986 835980
www.trulytraceable.com

Tuckers Butchers - Mumbles
Swansea
01792 850084

Turners Game Poultry & Meats
Canterbury
01227 722249
www.turnersgame.co.uk

Upton Smokery
Oxfordshire
www.uptonsmokery.co.uk

Wild And Game
Bristol
0800 4334334
www.wildandgame.co.uk

Willo Game
Bishops Castle
01588 650119
www.willogame.co.uk

Audi Q4 e-tron

The pioneering electric drive of e-tron, the unmistakable design aesthetic of Audi: both come together in Audi's first compact, fully electric SUV. Available in two body styles, the Q4 e-tron is now available to order, with the Q4 Sportback e-tron due later this year.

Their road space requirements make them versatile and agile all-rounders, yet their interior space is far from compact - offering unrestricted space and comfort comparable to a full-size SUV.

Bristol Audi

Audi e-tron GT

The Audi e-tron GT quattro and Audi RS e-tron GT are now available to test drive. Combining electric car efficiency with the legendary performance and aesthetics of Audi Sport, they take their place at the top of our fully-electric line-up.

With separate motors driving each axle, power is evenly distributed. And with adaptive air suspension, rear wheel steering, sports differential and electronic torque vectoring all as standard on the RS e-tron GT, handling is as exhilarating as accelerating. Be it the country side or the city, the e-tron GT is ready to take you everywhere.

Game & Wine Pairing

There are careful considerations to be made when pairing wine with game. Often game can be an overpowering flavour and usually served with an even richer sauce to accompany it so try to understand which are the boldest flavours in the dish and pair against those. White wines are often overlooked when pairing wine with game but a rich, full bodied white wine with game can work wonderfully well.

Venison Epigrams by Jose Souto

Rioja Reserva *Spain*

The breadcrumbs in this dish give an added layer of flavour and texture that should be considered when pairing a wine.

The oak of a Rioja would cut right through beautifully and allow for both of the rich flavours to sing. Rioja often has notes of mulberries and cherry that pair well with venison.

Rioja Reserva *Selected Red wines of the best vintages with an excellent potential that have been aged for a minimum of 3 years, with at least one year in casks. This is where Rioja tastes serious. At the Reserva level, winemakers often age their wines longer than the minimum and select better grapes.*

Roast Loin of Roe Deer by Hywel Griffith

Chassagne Montrachet *France*

The beautiful creamy sauce that accompanies this dish could potentially overwhelm a wine particularly as Jerusalem Artichokes are tricky to pair wines to.

An oaked Chardonnay will be a stunning accompaniment to compliment this dish. Try a Chassagne Montrachet or a big bold Californian Chardonnay.

Chassagne Montrachet *When it comes to the world's greatest white wines, the border between Chassagne and Puligny is the treasure at the end of the rainbow. Within a few hundred metres lie five wonderful Grands Crus, three of which are in Chassagne. They are led by the luscious Le Montrachet, to which Chassagne gained permission in 1879, along with Puligny, to hyphenate its name.*

Venison Wellington with New Potatoes & Buttered Baby Carrots
by Gary Maclean

Red Bordeaux – Saint-Émilion *France*

A classic dish such as this deserves a classic wine. As the main grape variety in Saint-Émilion is Merlot the wine will be a little softer than other Bordeaux's and compliment the Venison well.

The lean protein of the Venison will eliminate the tannins in the wine and allow the beautiful hedgerow fruit to come through.

Saint-Émilion *is a key wine town in the Libournais district of Bordeaux, important in terms of both quality and quantity. It lies just a few miles north of the Dordogne, in the final stages of the river's journey from the hills of the Massif Central to the Gironde estuary. The town is renowned as much for its beautiful buildings and scenery as for its wine. Its steep, narrow, cobbled streets, overlooked by its Romanesque church and the iconic 13th-century Tour du Roy tower are a reminder of the town's long history..*

Pheasant 'Maryland' by Glynn Purnell

Chateau Musar *Lebanon* **or Californian Cabernet Sauvignon**

With the big flavours of the pheasant and the fantastic use of aromatics in this dish you will need a wine that can stand its ground and work in harmony.

Chateau Musar from Lebanon is a robust wine that adds depth of flavour, a touch of spice of and is fragranced with dark fruits that will beautifully draw out the Cajun spice and ginger from the pheasant. If you can't find this specific wine, try a full bodied Cabernet Sauvignon from California.

Chateau Musar *Think Bordeaux meets Arabian Nights, Chateau Musar's indulgent, sensuous flavours make it an unforgettable experience. It is also a testament to wine making passion, dedication and bravery in the face of a 15-year civil war.*

Cabernet Sauvignon *is dry and full-bodied, and is prized for its long aging potential. ... It's also known for displaying characteristic green flavours like bell pepper, eucalyptus and mint.*

Half Roasted Partridge, White Bean, Wild Mushrooms by Ian Gibbs

Condrieu *France*

The creamy texture of the white beans and wild mushrooms in this sauce require a wine that will lift the palate so avoid anything too acidic.

Condrieu from Northern Rhone is made from 100% Viognier grapes and often has notes of white peach and apricot and is low in acidity which would work well with this beautifully creamy sauce.

Condrieu *is arguably the northern Rhône's most distinctive wine appellation. Created in 1940, it covers white wines made exclusively from Viognier. In contrast, its larger neighbours (Saint-Joseph, Crôzes-Hermitage and Côte Rôtie) specialize in robust reds made from Syrah.*

Venison Wellington by Charlotte Vincent

Gevrey Chambertin *France*

The warm raspberry and blackcurrant fruits from this wine will not fail to impress with a classic Venison Wellington.

The lighter tannins of the wine will melt away when paired with the lean venison and will be even further enhanced if served with the suggested redcurrant and game jus.

Gevrey-Chambertin *is a village Côte de Nuits area, just North of Chambolle-Musigny in Burgundy, France, famous for producing praised Pinot Noir red wines. Gevrey-Chambertin gives birth to some of the world's most prestigious and expensive red wines in fact.*

Wine pairing created by Amy Hollier, a former operations manager at Simpsons restaurant in Edgbaston and a food service lecturer at University College Birmingham who takes wine studies and a senior role in training budding waiters and waitresses in front of house service.

Check out her 'Wine Find' app to pair a wine for almost every conceivable dish.

Amy Hollier

Wine Expert, Educator & Author

Photo credit: @themiscellanista - Unsplash

ESTABLISHED 1935

Recognisably Different

FOXDENTON
SPIRITS & LIQUEURS

Cocktails

These cocktails have all been mixed using flavours that perfectly compliment game. Hedgerow fruits such as blackberries and sloes have been used to warm up and give classics such as a Negroni and Bramble a twist. Apricot and almond have been chosen to complement feathered game such as grouse and pheasant.

Amy Hollier
Wine Expert, Educator & Author

Sloe Gin Negroni

25ml Foxdenton Sloe Gin Liqueur
25ml Campari
25ml Orange & Rosemary Gin Liqueur
Rosemary for garnish

Pour all ingredients into a mixing glass with ice and stir. Strain into a rocks glass with a large sphere of ice. Garnish with a sprig of rosemary.

Bramble

50 ml Foxdenton Raspberry Gin Liqueur
25ml Foxdenton Gin
15ml Crème de Mure
15ml Lemon Juice
15ml Sugar Syrup
Blackberry for garnish

Add all ingredients to a cocktail shaker with ice. Shake well and strain into a rocks glass filled with crushed ice. Drizzle the Crème de Mure down one side of the glass. Garnish with a blackberry.garnish with a cherry.

Apricot and Amaretto Sour

75ml Amaretto
25ml Foxdenton Golden Apricot Gin Liqueur
25ml Lemon Juice
1 Egg White
Cherry for garnish

Add the ingredients to a cocktail shaker filled with ice and shake well. Pour into a tumbler and garnish with a cherry.

English Garden Martini

75ml Foxdenton English Garden Distilled Gin
25ml Dry Vermouth

Pour the vermouth into a mixing glass with ice, stir and strain it off to leave the ice cubes coated in vermouth. Pour over the gin and stir for 30 seconds. Strain into a chilled martini glass.

Lashings of....

50ml Foxdenton Rhubarb Gin Liqueur
30ml Apple Juice
Ginger Beer

Fill a tall glass with ice and pour over the Liqueur and apple juice before topping up with Ginger Beer. Stir and then garnish with a slither of apple.

game facts

Snipe hunting is the most difficult of all game shoots. Snipes have no protection from trees or bushes to use to their advantage and must rely on sheer speed to get airborne. Their zig zagging makes them particularly hard to shoot.

The fastest game bird is the **red grouse** that can reach speeds of 63 mph.

The **red grouse** is the bird featured on the Famous Grouse whisky bottle. Invented in 1896 and named after a Scottish bird. The famous label was added due to the popularity of grouse.

To hang or not to hang?

Game flavour increases with hanging the birds with the carcass in. Older generations revered this richer flavour but it is not as popular with today's chefs who prefer a younger, fresher flavour that goes better with younger wines.

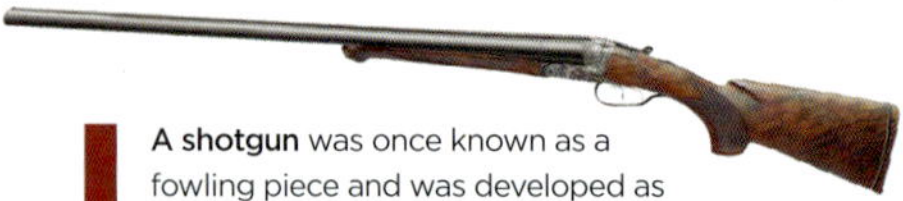

A shotgun was once known as a fowling piece and was developed as a long-barrelled firearm designed to shoot a straight-walled cartridge known as a shotshell.

Rabbits and hares are herbivorous mammals of the order Lagomorpha. Britain's only native member of the group is the mountain hare (Lepus timidus). Both the rabbit and the brown hare were introduced.

Red deer have been depicted in cave art from as early as 40,000 years ago during the Upper Paleolithic period.

The pheasant prefers to run and only flies to escape. It's preferred habitat is undisturbed grass

Woodcock is traditionally roasted and served with the head, feet and guts left in tact. The guts liquidise during cooking to produce the sauce.

Chefs prefer the **grey legged partridge** for its texture and flavour and it is much rarer than the red legged variety that comes from Spain and France.

AUGUST
12

Glorious Twelfth

The **12th of August**, commonly celebrated as the Glorious Twelfth, which was enshrined in law in the **1831 Game Act** and marks the start of the British game shooting season. It declares the **Red Grouse**, a medium sized and much-prized bird unique to Northern England and Scotland, as fair game, meaning it could not be shot before then. This is one of the busiest days in the shooting season.

Why you should eat game meat

It is Healthy! One of the main benefits of eating game meat is that is it one of the most healthiest meats available, very low in fat and cholesterol, game meat is lean as they are wild and are able to walk and roam freely so do not store so much fat.

- The fat that is in game meat is Omega 3 When you hear Omega-3, most people will think of salmon, however wild game such as venison has an optimum ratio of Omega-3 to Omega-6 fatty acids, making game one of the healthiest sources of good fat.
- Game is very high in Iron and contains higher levels of many beneficial nutrients including vitamin E, Beta Carotene, Zinc Vitamin B(6) and Selenium. Selenium is an important part of our diet that we often lack and helps protect cells from damage caused by free radicals.
- Wild game is ideal for those following a paleo approach to eating and for those wishing to lose weight as it has fewer calories than other meats. Venison is high in protein good for high protein diets
- All game is hormone free no growth hormones are added to their diets as their diets are natural
- Wild game such as venison, rabbit, pigeon and grouse are antibiotic-free.

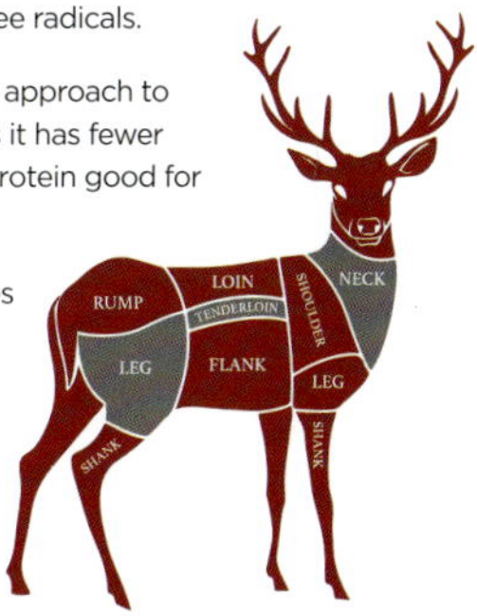

Source: https://tasteofgame.org.uk

the great game guide

2021/22

Offers & Vouchers